TRUST THE FLOW

Awakening with Kambo, Cannabis and Ayahuasca

by Tara Rose

TABLE OF CONTENTS

AUTHOR'S NOTE

This is a work of nonfiction. In some cases throughout this book, I use pseudonyms to protect the privacy of people I write about, especially if they were engaged in potentially illegal activities. Generally it will be obvious in the text when this is the case. No other facts were altered.

Also, I sometimes use the term "Spirit" throughout this book, and by that, I mean to indicate the benevolent, intelligent force behind all that is.

PART I: INITIATIONS INTO PURPOSE

1

AYAHUASCA

S ome people book flights to the Amazon when they want to drink ayahuasca. Others post surreptitiously on internet forums to try and find it in the underground.

I do things differently.

"Ayahuasca, I would like to meet you," I said. "Please come and find me."

When you seek the company of an omniscient being, a sincere invitation is all that is needed to open the door.

After all, ayahuasca – the potent, purgative brew known for producing profound, life-changing visions – originated as a shamanic medicine used by the healers of Amazonian villages and tribes for divination and for diagnostic purposes. They would drink ayahuasca to get instructions from the spirits about how to heal a patient who was ill in body, mind or spirit, as well as, sometimes, to facilitate that healing while connected, through the medicine's influence, to the visionary realms. Ayahuasca was their way of accessing the world-wide web of the ethers. It is a portal to other dimensions, a source of magic, and a way to talk with the ancestors.

Ayahuasca is typically made from a vine that grows in the Amazon jungle, *Banisteriopsis caapi*, mixed with the leaves of the chacruna plant, *Psychotria viridis*, although there are other variations that use acacia bark from *Mimosa hostilis*. Both formulations contain the psychoactive chemical DMT, a compound linked to mystical experiences which naturally exists within the human brain, and is endogenous to the brains of all mammals. Ingesting the brew produces profound, mind-bending journeys that last six to eight hours.

I was very intrigued by the prospect of meeting such a powerful teacher as ayahuasca. Her spirit is considered to be an emanation of the Earth herself, Gaia, as well as the Cosmic Mother, the feminine half of God.

Shortly after I invited ayahuasca into my life, I attended a networking event for intuitive energy healers, and that's where I met a dark-skinned Native American man with light brown eyes that seemed to have an otherworldly glow about them.

"Well hello, star being," I said to him. He laughed and smiled widely, looking pleased to be recognized.

"Let's have tea and find out why we're drawn to each other," he said.

At a cafe, we ran through a checklist of reasons why the Universe might have put us in each other's paths. Was one of us supposed to heal the other? No, that didn't resonate. Was one of us supposed to teach the other? No, that wasn't it either.

"I wrote a book called *Dandelion Hunter*. It's about my experiences using wild plants for food and medicine in Portland, and meditating with them," I told him, wondering if that might lead us to a clue.

It did. He said he was a plant medicine enthusiast too, and that in fact he was getting ready to attend an ayahuasca ceremony facilitated by a healer he deeply respected. And did I want to join him?

"Yes!" I said.

I had been curious about ayahuasca ever since I read about the profound visionary experiences it bestows in Daniel Pinchbeck's

2003 book, *Breaking Open the Head: A Psychedelic Journey into the Heart of Contemporary Shamanism.*

As an herbalist, I had learned to meditate with wild plants and listen to their wisdom. Yogis have human gurus that teach and guide them. But in many indigenous traditions, and for me, the gurus are the plants, the most ancient of Earth's living beings. For those in the Amazon, ayahuasca is the queen of them all.

And yet, while this medicine is a holy sacrament to those who drink it, the American government has made possession of ayahuasca a felony. For this reason, if I wanted to attend, my new friend explained, I would have to agree to keep my participation a secret, the identity of the facilitator a secret, and the identity of all participants a secret, too.

"No problem," I said.

The organizers put me through a vetting process to make sure they felt comfortable trusting me. This involved meeting them in person, with my new friend present and vouching for my sincerity, and then submitting an extensive written questionnaire discussing my intentions and my history with regard to psychedelics, spirituality, physical and mental health. This was given to the shaman who would be facilitating the ceremony, so that he could get to know me as well.

This person who would lead my first ceremony is a respected author and transformational life coach who went to the jungle to get trained and initiated in the ways of the Shipibo people of Peru, an indigenous group with an ancestral tradition of working with ayahuasca. My friend spoke highly of him.

When he called me to talk on the phone for the first time, I said, "I realize that we've never met and I don't know what you look like, but I recently had a dream that you told me, 'Trust the medicine.'"

"That *is* something I would say," he replied.

A good omen, for sure.

For the time ahead of this eight-hour meditation ceremony, I did all I could to prepare.

As an offering, I sent energy blessings of love and deep respect to the spirit of ayahuasca.

I practiced sitting still and breathing into my heart, for that is the place our consciousness must be in order to hear the spirit world. And I observed the strict dietary restrictions that were sent out to all of the participants: no dairy, no sugar, no sodium, no spices, no coffee, no alcohol, no cannabis, nor processed foods for at least two weeks ahead of the ceremony.

The location of the ceremony was secret, only revealed in a secure communication right before the event. We were reminded in this missive to fast from food several hours before the ceremony and wear all-white clothing at the event in order to attract light, positive energy.

When I arrived at the address, I found that it was a mansion. People were milling about outside on the grounds, soaking up the sunlight. I saw a group of about thirty people ranging in age from mid-twenties to gray hair. Almost all of them were strangers to me.

The ceremony space was a huge interior room with all the furniture removed. Everyone had brought meditation cushions and blankets which they made into little nests lining the perimeter of the walls.

We had been given pre-arranged seating in a placement designed by the shaman to balance the energies of the group. I discovered I had been placed at the edge of the gender split, the last woman next to the men and directly across from the shaman leading the ceremony.

Each seat had a little plastic "purge bucket" and some paper towels next to it in case we might vomit. This made me nervous.

"Is it hard to hear people getting sick around you?" I asked someone.

"They're not getting sick. They're getting well," he replied.

He meant that vomiting in ceremony is a form of catharsis, a way of releasing emotional, spiritual, and physical toxins. Still, I felt apprehensive. I had only thrown up a couple times in childhood and hoped it wouldn't happen.

As we waited for the ceremony to begin I felt caught between dueling emotions of excitement and anxiety. The comforting voice of a close friend popped into my mind then, saying, as he often did when I had a fear of the unknown: "Could it be fun?"

At dusk, the shaman took his seat at the front of the room. It was impressive, with a banner of a jaguar posted up behind him and a white, sheepskin rug at his feet. He was tall, dark-haired and broad-shouldered, with handsome looks. He reminded me of a Disney prince, like Aladdin. He had a very serious demeanor, more than a little bit intimidating.

A man and a woman flanked him on either side. They were sound healers and also assistants designated to help anyone who needed physical or emotional support during the ceremony if the facilitator was occupied.

"Whatever you think is going to happen tonight, that is not what's going to happen," the shaman said.

He told us to trust the journey, to reach out for help only as a last resort, and to remember to communicate directly with the plant spirit if we wanted things to be gentler at any point because ayahuasca, whom he called *Madre*, would adjust our experience accordingly.

Then we went around the room and everyone introduced themselves by first name only and talked about their intentions. I said, "I'm here to meet the plant spirit, but also, I'm tired of playing whack-a-mole with fear. Fear of this, fear of that." I wondered if ayahuasca could get rid of the chronic anxiety I was so tired of wrestling with.

The lights were turned off, candles lit, and the shaman poured the medicine into tiny teacups. He called each of us up to the front of the room to receive our dose as he blessed it.

"Make relations with the medicine," he said to us.

We looked at it, dabbed our fingers into it, and inhaled the cloyingly sweet scent of this viscous, maroon colored substance, which looked a lot like blood.

Once everyone had been served, it was time for us to drink together. We raised our glasses and said *"Salud!"* The flavor was slightly reminiscent of anise, I thought. But I saw other people twisting up their faces in ways that suggested it was highly unpleasant to their palate, perhaps sickeningly sweet or bitter.

We sat in darkness and silence together then, the candles blown out, waiting to feel the medicine take effect.

I started to feel warm and relaxed. I sighed deeply. Beautiful, strange melodies twirled through the air, propelled by exotic musical instruments and words in languages I had never heard before.

A vision materialized behind my closed eyes. I was an infant, a little baby very lovingly swaddled in the arms of a dark-skinned, large-bosomed woman, *Madre*, the spirit of the brew. As she held me it felt like a great homecoming, like she already knew me better than anyone I had ever met, and her affection for me was so great, so fulfilling and so deep, that it washed over me like a wave that poured love into every cell of my being. I felt a profound sense of safety and security in her arms, unlike I'd ever felt before. It was bliss.

The imagery appearing was sensuously beautiful and intricate. It looked like a vivid series of paintings that had been rendered in an African style, with deep, rich colors of wine red and rust.

Madre held me in her arms in a landscape of rolling, sand colored hills. Off in the distance I saw two ogres lumbering towards us, with the intent to threaten me. But instead of frightening, it just struck me as silly. What harm could any monster do to me with God Herself holding me like that? The bravado of it was so absurd that I couldn't help but laugh. And what a relief it was to laugh!

The shaman called each of us forward, one by one, for personal blessings and healings. We were supposed to crawl to him because walking was too difficult to do under the influence of ayahuasca. I felt disconnected from my body and I struggled to figure out how to use my arms and legs, so I attempted to crawl and then I stopped.

You weren't supposed to talk, but I did. I said, "Can someone help me out? I feel like I'm stuck in eternity here." The room erupted in laughter. It was too true!

One of the assistants came and guided me forward to the front of the room, to stand on my knees on a cushion in front of the shaman. This shaman – whom I will call Maestro, because that is what his assistants called him – poured a fragrant liquid called *Agua de Florida* into my hands and told me to rub them together and then place one on my heart and one on my belly. Then I knelt before him and he played a melody over me and while he did, a powerful vision appeared.

I was on stage in a huge stadium, standing at a podium. Before me was a vast crowd, an audience of billions of cosmic beings, all of whom were looking upon me with deep respect. I felt as if I were being honored.

I had the distinct impression that they all knew who I was. It seemed as if I were some kind of massively famous public figure to them, a celebrity in the spirit world.

But why? I wondered. *Who am I?*

2

MY NAME

After the ceremony, the question remained: *Who am I?*

Certainly I had long lamented my given name: Rebecca Elizabeth Lerner. I cringe even to write it. It is very irritating to me, because it is so incongruous with my spirit. I wanted a name that resonated with my soul and reflected it through sound.

For many years I used the nickname "Becky" because it felt at least less stodgy and formal than "Rebecca," but that was still only a placeholder, something tolerable to go by until I found my true name.

It was a long wait. When I tried to brainstorm options, nothing ever came to mind that felt right.

Eventually it occurred to me that I had been going about it all wrong. I had been trying to find myself through thinking. But if I really wanted to discover my true identity, then what I needed to do was consult the very core of my being, my soul. And the doorway to the soul isn't the mind. It's the heart.

The heart opens when it is given loving presence, stillness, and receptivity.

So, I closed my eyes and placed my hands on my heart, relaxing inwardly as I cultivated gentle feelings of loving kindness and respect. I directed this warm, glowing offering to the center of my heart. When it opened, I tuned in further with my awareness until I could feel the energetic essence within myself, my soul. When I felt thoroughly connected to this most inward part of my being, I silently asked the question: "What is my true name?"

I sat then in stillness, waiting for an answer to arise. Would there even be an answer at all? What if silence was the answer? And if there was a sound, would it be in a language I understood? What if my true name was in an African click language or something? Would I be able to repeat it? If I heard it, would I like it?

Eventually my thoughts subsided, and then an image appeared: A dark-haired woman sitting with a straight back upon a lotus flower. She looked exactly like me, only more regal. And then I received an auditory message, a sound: "Tara," pronounced with a long "A." Tah-rah.

So I did have a name after all!

This one was unexpected. I had never considered the name Tara before. It had never been a thought. Yet I liked the sound of it very much, actually.

I recalled vaguely that it had some kind of significance among the Eastern traditions – maybe Hindu, perhaps?

I consulted Google, the all-knowing oracle of our time, and then I learned that indeed, "Tara" is a Sanskrit word meaning *star*. And in Tibetan Buddhism, Tara is also the name of a female buddha, a fully awakened being and spiritual master who guides her devotees to enlightenment from the celestial realms of Heaven, where she sits upon a lotus-flower throne.

In fact Tara is not just a buddha, but also a savior and a deity. She is a sacred embodiment of God in feminine form. She is revered throughout Asia, and the broader Buddhist diaspora, as a goddess of compassion and wisdom. It is said that she works tirelessly to liberate humanity from suffering using her karmic merit earned by doing many great and heroic deeds. For instance, she is said to have meditated for a million years while emanating illuminated frequencies so that other beings could catch enlightenment vibes while wading through the murky waters of incarnation.

People also pray to her because she is a powerful protector from the forces of *Mara*. *Mara* is the Buddhist name for the great demon who keeps us caught in illusions, addictions, attachments and otherwise stuck, distracted or disconnected from our path of awakening – sort of like the Christian concept of Satan. In Hinduism, Tara is depicted as a particularly fierce warrior goddess.

Interestingly, in these traditions, Tara is not just a deity; she is known to incarnate on Earth as a human being as well. She has had many, many lifetimes here on Earth with which to attain her great wisdom and compassion.

In one famous story, Tara was born as a princess. Her parents, the king and queen, wanted her to get married and have a conventional life, but she rebelled. Instead of doing traditional princess things, she preferred to devote herself to spiritual pursuits. She spent all her time with Buddhist monks, learning their teachings and meditating with them at the local monastery. The monks were very impressed with her. They appreciated her sincerity and devotion. That's why they told her, "We will pray for you to be reborn as a man. That way, you can attain enlightenment."

"Nonsense," Tara replied. "I will incarnate as a woman when I achieve buddhahood to prove to the world that a woman is just as capable as a man."

I liked that. I liked it a lot.

There was just one problem: Tara is only one word. "What is my last name?" I wondered. "I'm not Madonna."

I asked the Universe to grace me with an answer, and some time later a reply came to me in the form of the image of a wild rose blossom in my mind's eye, pink with five petals and a yellow center. Rose. I loved it, and not just because the flower is beautiful to look at. In plant spirit medicine, the rose embodies the energetic frequency of unconditional love.

And that's the story of how I became Tara Rose.

3

SPIRALS

I watched as Maestro and his assistants took turns blowing an herbal snuff up each other's noses with a long bamboo pipe. They winced and smacked their knees as it traveled up their air passages, and then they wretched and coughed and vomited, rather violently.

When he saw me watching, Maestro said, "You can have some later."

"I'm not sure I want that," I whispered to the woman sitting next to me, who had partaken. "What is it?"

"Hapé," she said, pronounced like *HAHP-ay*.

"It looks painful," I said.

"It clears you out," she said.

"Is it like snorting wasabi?" I asked.

She laughed. "Kind of."

Hapé, I would later learn, is an Amazonian medicine made of the ritually burned ashes of tobacco, *Nicotiana rustica*, mixed with a variety of other herbs in proprietary blends unique to each maker. Many people like to use it before working with ayahuasca because it opens your channel to spirit while also centering you, purifying your system and grounding your energy into the Earth, and that is an excellent place to start from when you are about to embark on an expansive visionary journey.

Within the shamanic traditions of South America, hapé is also used as a tool for shamanic activation, because as a master blows the medicine into the student, he is transferring some of his spirit, his magical essence, through the breath, and in this way can also transmit vibrational gifts.

I was one of the eight *"pasajeros"* who had traveled to this plywood shack in the high desert landscape of eastern Oregon, off the grid, to drink another dose of the magical tea of the vine. We sat in a circle on a concrete floor with our backs upright in meditation chairs, our legs splayed out comfortably on our blankets and pillows. Outside, the moon was visible in the sky and the desert stars sparkled over the landscape.

Maestro lit a tea-light candle. He sat with assistants on either side of him. It was a cozy group. He opened with a pep talk of sorts, reminding us that whatever happened would be perfect and divinely guided – but also unpredictable.

"If you get into a tough spot, ask the *Madre* for help before you ask one of us," he said. She is a conscious and sentient being who wants us to learn and receive healing from her, and she can make things harder or easier for us in the moment.

When it was time to set our intentions and share them aloud, I said, "I want to learn how to heal the Earth."

"You think you can just walk in here and learn that? That's a path. It takes years to learn. Heal the Earth in your body. Your body is made of Earth," Maestro replied.

"Aho," the others said in response. This is a Native American word that means something like "amen."

When it was time to serve the medicine, Maestro called each of us up by name to receive our individual doses in tiny clear tea cups.

Before pouring it he looked at me very closely, reading my energy and intuiting the amount I needed as he meticulously measured the dose. Then he raised his eyebrow to silently ask me if I concurred with his assessment. I was struck by his careful movements and immense attention to detail during this process. Everything he did, even wiping drops of medicine off the bottle with a paper towel, he did with his full, undivided presence and a feeling of great love.

"No wonder they call him the master," I thought.

He was currently abstaining from all human touch, he told us, because his teacher in the Amazon, a master shaman named Ricardo, had asked that of him. I knew he had also been a student of don Oscar Miro-Quesada, an author, world-renowned Peruvian curandero and creator of the cross-cultural Pachakuti Mesa shamanic tradition. (Maestro looks a bit like don Oscar, too.)

As we raised our glasses together, we made a toast. We said, *"Aho, Mitakuye Oyasin,"* which means, "Respect, to all my relations." It is an affirmation of our oneness with all beings, from the birds to the stars, the grass and the rivers.

When I swallowed the syrupy liquid, I expected something blissful to happen, like my first time drinking the medicine.

That is not what happened. As the psychoactive component came on, I felt sharp pains in my heart and solar plexus, and a feeling of being very alone, exposed and vulnerable.

"Receive the medicine," I heard Maestro say to the group.

I wanted to surrender to the discomfort, relax and let go, but I couldn't do it. I felt afraid. I tried to think my way through it, to persuade myself that fear was irrational, but that didn't work. For hours I was stuck in my head, wrestling with fear and losing the battle. Eventually, I asked for help.

Maestro directed me to sit in front of his assistant. I scooted across the concrete floor towards the sound of her hand patting a cushion. She began to sing a beautiful song to me, but it did not help because I could not stop the incessant spiraling of thoughts and the feeling of fear. I really wanted to sink into magic and have a visionary experience, and I felt very frustrated that I could not manage to break through this wall. The rest of the night, I suffered.

The next morning, Maestro led a group integration circle in which we were invited to share our experiences. When I told everyone what I had gone through, I felt embarrassed and ashamed that I had failed to do something as simple as let go. Why couldn't I?

"When the mind spirals, it's because there is a block of energy in the heart," Maestro said. "There's something you're not facing."

I wondered what it was.

"There is something here. If there was, what would it be?" Maestro asked me.

This was a very uncomfortable question. I did not want to explore my innermost feelings, especially in front of other people. I wanted to feel strong, and at that time I confused stoicism for strength.

"It isn't 'more spiritual' to avoid your feelings," Maestro said. "The keys to this path are sincerity and vulnerability. Go into your heart and be with that. Feel it."

It was so intimidating to do that in front of everyone, but I could see that if I didn't, I would only stay stuck. So I did it. I felt the pain inside my heart, and tears came out. I covered my face.

"Good," he said. "Now that the energy has moved you won't be stuck in your head."

"I'm worried that maybe this happened because I didn't meditate enough before the ceremony," I said.

"If you believe in punishment, that's because of your conditioning," Maestro replied. "What would God say to you?"

"I don't know," I said.

"Don't try to think about it," Maestro said. "What's the first thing that comes to you? What would God say to you right now?"

"I'm fine? It's fine?" I answered.

"Yes, you're fine," he said.

"Do you think this happened on purpose?" I asked.

"What would God say about that?" Maestro asked me again.

"Trust?" I said.

"Yes, trust," he said. "If you're suffering, it means you're believing something that isn't true."

What unfolded next really surprised me. Two women sitting next to me shared that they had also spent the evening wrestling with overactive minds and feelings of anxiety. I had thought I was the only one, but I wasn't at all.

"It was a mental purge," one of the assistants said.

Outside in the desert, the sand was dotted with bright yellow rabbit sage and scraggly, splitting juniper trees, and piles of huge, people-sized rocks. I walked to the fire that was now smoldering but had been burning all night long, and I thought back to a conversation with an apprentice whom I had trained in plant spirit meditation, Matthew. He had had a vision while communing with a non-psychoactive tincture of elderberry in a plant spirit meditation ceremony.

"Elves were handing me presents, and inside each box was a life experience," Matthew had said. "Then they showed me a beach filled with grains of sand, and they said, 'Pick out the bad ones.'"

"What do you think it meant?" I had asked.

"That you can't," he said. "All experiences have value."

On the second night of our journey, Maestro passed around a jar of mapacho, sacred Amazon tobacco, and told us all to take a pinch of it and then go outside and offer it in gratitude to Pachamama, by placing it lovingly in the desert outside the rustic cob homestead we were in, our little cave.

"The Native American cultures I have studied with teach that all plants come from the stars except for tobacco. Tobacco is the only plant native to Earth," Maestro said.

When it came time for us to prepare for the medicine again and set intentions, I felt humbled. "My intention is to be present for whatever *La Madre* wants to show me," I said.

I hoped I would not spend another night wrestling with my ego. I watched my breath go in and out. At the bottom of the exhale, there was a subtle feeling of peace. I sank into it.

Maestro whispered to the cup he had filled with ayahuasca, chanting words in another language. He handed it to me, and I went back to my seat, my nest of blankets and pillows. I drank my dose and sat in darkness, and silence, waiting for the effects to come on. The roller coaster ratcheted up the track.

I imagined that the energy in my body was grounding down deep into the Earth through my seat. I focused inward, bringing my awareness into my heart space, intending my consciousness to merge with that of the medicine's spirit.

The music began. I heard a didgeridoo, and then a flute. I felt the presence of the plant spirit guide my hands together in a prayer position in front of my heart. "Thank you," I said silently. And then I dove into this feeling of gratitude, amplifying it.

As I did this, my heart softened. Apprehension melted, and there was a sense of peace and lightness. With my eyes open I saw wisps of pastel pink and blue energy swirling through the ceremony space like smoke.

"Receive," I heard Maestro say to the room. "Receive the medicine. Let it heal you. Take it deep into your heart and soul."

I felt like a small child listening to lullabies. The notes of the flute playing made colors change in the air.

I regressed even younger to become a tiny baby with a mind that does not yet fully function – I suspected I was perhaps even a fetus – yet I was surprised that I still had a very keen awareness. I had thought such beings would be too primitive to understand what is happening around them, but upon experiencing it again, I realized that that is not true. I felt very perceptive and fully conscious, immensely aware of my vulnerability and afraid of the physical world. I needed some reassurance. I wanted to feel protected by my mother's own strength, to sense her peace and trust in life. I wanted to feel enveloped by her love and warmth and serenity, but I did not feel it. I felt nothing. I felt unmet. I felt alone. Mom was extremely anxious herself.

This mother was not the plant spirit, not *Madre Ayahuasca*, but rather my human mom, Sheila, the woman who gave birth to me in this lifetime. And so as my tiny neural network developed into a brain, I was imprinted with fear, and the core belief that life is dangerous.

Now I could understand why anxiety had plagued me so incessantly in this life, and why it had been so hard to overcome, even when I knew it was irrational. It had been there from the very beginning, I now understood.

Words hissed through my being. A serpent spoke, saying, *"Forgive Sheila."*

"Forgive Sheila," I heard, again, and again, as *Madre* gently nudged me to use this new insight to find compassion for her limitations, rather than blame.

"No *negativo*," I heard the shaman's assistant chanting, waving his hands. He was shooing away negative energies, negative entities.

"We stay healthy by staying in harmony with the cycles of nature, and connecting with Spirit. The Earth is our mother," I heard Maestro say.

"The sun is one of billions or trillions of other creative energies shining out on the Universe and the same intelligence that makes flowers makes stars and makes people," he said.

It seemed he was programming our subconscious minds, helping us to remember what we are doing here on this planet, and to remain in awe of it. How easily we can forget.

"The shaman is calling you," I heard the person next to me say.

I crawled across the floor to sit in front of Maestro. He played beautiful melodies from his flute, and then he leaned in and whispered to me, "Tara, become the medicine. Live it. Embody it, and model it for others. Keep connecting to Earth energy, plant energy, embodying it and sharing it."

Back at my seat, my mind slipped into chatter. Maestro called me back to sit in front of him.

"You're still in the struggle between your mind and your heart. Are you aware of this?" he asked.

"Yes," I said.

"You need to be vigilant and not slide backwards into your old ways when you leave here. Do you understand?"

"Yes," I said.

I resolved to try.

4

HAPÉ DREAMS

The first time I experienced hapé medicine was in a dream. I was technically asleep when I found myself seated inside a candlelit cave across from Maestro, the ayahuasca shaman.

He said to me, "What do you need?"

"I don't know," I replied.

"Hapé," he said.

My heart leapt a bit in fear of the burning sensation I thought I would feel in my sinuses if the tobacco snuff was blown into them. But before I could protest, Maestro placed a wooden pipe at the base of my nostril and sent the medicine flowing gently into my brain with love.

The effect was swift: My spirit shot up into outer space with great velocity, like a rocket, and then I was flying high and soaring through the glittering stars.

Clouds of space rocks hurtled towards me, but they did no harm because with the hapé, I was transcendent. My vibration was so extremely high and fast that nothing solid could touch me.

I awoke from the dream feeling awe.

I saw a very unusual license plate that said 77777 later that day. The repeating number 7 is an omen of soul purpose alignment. It happened to feature itself prominently in Maestro's email address, as well.

I took this as a sign from the Universe that my dream was not just a dream.

5

PROHIBITION

When I was a teenager, my friends and I would get together at a local pond and smoke blunts after school, trying to get as stoned as we possibly could, because that was as close to an adventure as we could get in suburbia. Sometimes we would "hotbox" their parents' minivans, sealing up the windows and puff-puff-passing the herb until the cloud we sat inside was so thick we couldn't see. The change in consciousness it created was exciting and novel. I remember my muscles felt so relaxed it seemed like my head could slide right off my neck. We'd sit there for hours listening to music. Sound had a greater depth and richness to it, and the melodies were dazzling to us in our altered state.

Experimenting with weed like that seemed very innocent to me, yet we did all of this at great personal risk, because it was illegal back then. We had to hide our weed from the police officers who patrolled the town and also conceal the smell from our parents, lest we face persecution on the homefront as well. This wasn't always easy.

One day, as I sat at the kitchen table, my mother walked over to where I was sitting, bent down to peer into my blazed and bloodshot eyes, and asked pointedly, with an air of great suspicion, "Why are your eyes so red?"

I was wearing a tie-dye T-shirt and reeking of skunky smoke after having just gone to a Dave Matthews Band concert, so I was a walking red flag for the ganj. Mom is highly intuitive and keenly perceptive, and thus very difficult to fool. But fortunately she is also highly averse to conflict. I tried to use that tendency to my advantage.

"Oh, are they red? Maybe it's allergies," I said, trying my best to seem nonchalant.

Mom raised an eyebrow, but rather than press the matter, she said nothing. I thought I had gotten away with it. But apparently not. Days later, when she was driving us to the mall to buy new school clothes, I lost the thread of our conversation because I had been smoking so much that my short-term memory was glitching. I had to ask her what we were talking about. Like a sniper waiting patiently for the moment to strike, Mom took aim. She deadpanned: "Moderation, Becky. Moderation."

There was a weekend evening when I came home from a party very high and absolutely reeking of pot. As soon as I opened the front door I immediately rushed up the stairs to my bedroom, hoping to avoid interacting with my parents in such a state. Unfortunately for me, Dad's suspicions were immediately piqued and he charged up the stairs after me in a fury, chasing me to my room and pounding on my locked door. When I refused to open it, he started yelling. He kept up the barrage for an interminable amount of time. When he finally stopped and walked away, I breathed a sigh of relief, but then he called my phone over and over. My heart raced as it rang and rang all night long. In the morning, when I eventually found the courage to leave my bedroom and walk to the kitchen, he ambushed me and threatened to call the cops on my friends. Dad thought that by coming down hard on me like that, he was doing the right thing and protecting me from the danger of illegal drugs. But to me, weed was harmless, and his wrath was the most dangerous thing about it.

This was the late Nineties in suburban New Jersey. Police officers came to our schools and lectured us about how weed was an evil "gateway drug" that would get us hooked, fry our teenage brains and lead us down a dark road that would inevitably end in a crack addiction, or if not that, then a lethal heroin overdose. We were warned to resist "peer pressure" from drug dealers pushing pot with evil intentions. TV commercials said much the same, and the propaganda effectively convinced many people, including apparently Mom and Dad, that it was a terrible, rotten substance that would destroy their daughter.

Where did all this nonsense come from? Why was such a gentle, harmless herb so completely misunderstood? Why was it illegal in the first place?

I decided to do some research. I discovered that until the early Twentieth Century, ganja was widely embraced by the American public as a medicinal herb, much as it is today. Prohibition only began in 1937, when Congress declared cannabis a dangerous substance and banned it. Why had lawmakers done that? What changed? The answer, according to the Drug Policy Alliance, a cannabis advocacy group, was racism. Prohibition was the result of a propaganda wave fueled by anti-immigrant sentiment and bigotry.

In the early 1900s just after the Mexican Revolution...[there was] an influx of immigration from Mexico into states like Texas and Louisiana...These new Americans brought with them their native language, culture and customs. One of these customs was the use of cannabis as a medicine and relaxant.

Mexican immigrants referred to this plant as 'marihuana.' While Americans were very familiar with 'cannabis' because it was present in almost all tinctures and medicines available at the time, the word 'marihuana' was a foreign term...

The demonization of the cannabis plant was an extension of the demonization of the Mexican immigrants...The idea was to have an excuse to search, detain and deport Mexican immigrants.

That excuse became marijuana. During hearings on marijuana law in the 1930s, claims were [also] made about marijuana's ability to cause men of color to become violent and solicit sex from white women. This imagery became the backdrop for the Marijuana Tax Act of 1937 which effectively banned its use and sales.

Prohibition confronted me personally during a late-night traffic stop in my early twenties, when I was on my way home from a friend's house after smoking quite a bit of weed. A jolt of adrenaline pulsed through my system as flashing lights appeared in my rearview mirror. I pulled over and rolled down the window. The cop said he stopped me for a tail light issue, but then his eye fell upon a bundle of dried herbs in the console (it was just mugwort for smudging energy) and he grew suspicious.

"Why are your eyes so red? Have you been smoking weed tonight?" the cop asked.

"No," I said. That wasn't true, but avoiding self-incrimination and preserving my freedom felt more important than radical honesty. And if I was still a wee bit stoned, I didn't see it as a problem. Like a lot of people, my view was that cannabis made me more conscious rather than less, and thus actually enhanced my safety while driving, rather than compromising it. Maybe it did.

In "Cannabis and Driving," a research paper published in the academic journal *Frontiers in Psychiatry*, the authors undertook a meta-analysis of the available research on cannabis and driving to see whether it actually causes impairment in a way similar to alcohol intoxication. They concluded that cannabis does not appear to correlate with an increased collision risk and does not impair driving in the way alcohol does. It does slow down reaction times, however researchers found that people who are high on cannabis also tend to overcompensate and drive even more carefully, which actually negates that effect. Further, they found that the acute high from ganja wears off after about forty minutes, and that law enforcement currently doesn't have a way to take that into effect when prosecuting people for driving while under the influence of cannabis. "The legal cart is currently significantly ahead of the scientific horse," the authors wrote.

Was it a good idea to drive slightly stoned? I wouldn't do it today. I don't even like driving while tired. But back then, I felt confident that it was a fine idea, and I viewed that police officer as a misguided interloper operating from an invalid set of beliefs that led to the needless oppression of good people. My mission this evening was solely to avoid getting snagged in that trap.

"My eyes are red because I have allergies," I replied, very carefully.

"You took a little while to respond to my question. Is that because you're high?" the cop asked.

"No, it's because I'm tired, because it's 2 a.m.," I said.

He persisted, attempting to snag me with trick questions like, "When's the last time you smoked pot?" ("Never.") And, "How old were you when you first smoked weed?" to which I replied facetiously, "Why officer, I don't even know what it looks like, for I've always been a nerd."

We laughed heartily and at the end of this ridiculous inquisition, he actually shook my hand with a twinkle in his eyes that seemed to say, "Well played, madam, well played," because we both knew it was all just a game. His job was to gather evidence, and my job was to protect myself and create reasonable doubt.

I was very fortunate in this instance. Traffic stops more innocent than mine have gone so notoriously badly for people with a darker skin color than I. Not only have they at times been tragically lethal, but statistics also show that people with African ancestry consume cannabis at the same rate as everybody else, yet they are imprisoned for it nearly four times as often as people labeled "white." In 2020 in New York City, ninety-four percent of the individuals arrested for weed were African American, according to a report by Legal Aid Society.

The situation reflects not just systemic racism, but also a vast and galling ignorance about the true nature of what cannabis truly is.

And what cannabis really is, is an entheogen.

Cannabis has had a long history of use in many cultural traditions across the world. In *The Vedas,* Hindu texts dated to 2000 BC, cannabis is listed as one of five sacred plants. The deity Shiva is associated with *bhang,* a traditional tea made of cannabis boiled in milk, with ginger and pepper spices added to it. Today in India, dreadlocked Hindu, Jain and yogic ascetics, called *sadhus,* still imbibe freely on the streets.

In China, the great Taoist sage Confucius talked about cannabis. It was listed in classic Chinese pharmacopeias such as the *Zheng Lei Ben Cao* of 1108 AD and *Wu Zang Lun*, a manuscript from the Tang Dynasty of 618-907 AD.

"It should be mentioned that in ancient China, as in most early cultures, medicine had its origin in magic. Medicine men were practicing magicians. The evidence...suggests that the medicinal use of the hemp plant was widely known to the Neolithic peoples of northeastern Asia and shamanism was especially widespread in this northern area and also in China, and Cannabis played an important part of its rituals. The great mobility of the nomadic tribes north of China apparently assisted the movement of the plant to western Asia and from there to India, where its use as an [entheogen] intensified," Hui-Lin Li said in an article published in the academic journal *Economic Botany* in 1974, "The Origin and Use of Cannabis in Eastern Asia Linguistic Cultural Implications."

In Nineteenth Century Africa, in the Congo, the Baluba people (also known as the Bena-Riamba) practiced a cannabis-centered spiritual tradition called Riamba, complete with nightly tribal smoking ceremonies, according to the book *The African Roots of Marijuana* by Chris S. Duvall.

In tropical Jamaica, Rastafarians view weed as a religious sacrament that brings them closer to Jah, or God, and they smoke in prayer, to raise their consciousness and commune with divine energy.

And yet in America, an appreciation for the entheogenic properties of cannabis is only just beginning.

6

THE MOON TRIBE

Inspired by the structure and reverence of Maestro's ayahuasca ceremonies, I wondered what it would feel like to approach cannabis, the "people's psychedelic," in a similar sort of way. Might we have mystical experiences? What might unfold?

To find out, I held some special gatherings on the new and full moons and invited a small, eclectic group of close friends who I knew were experienced with both weed and meditation. One guy was a Reiki master and Qi Gong teacher. Another had lived in a Buddhist monastery for a while, studied with a self-professed wizard, and was nine years into a vow of celibacy. There was a man who drank ayahuasca often as a sacrament, and a couple who practiced Celtic shamanism. We gathered informally but regularly, and took to calling ourselves the "Moon Tribe."

Reggae music set the mood as my friends and I passed around a colorful glass pipe, a gold-infused bubbler filled with dried passionflower, the Blue Dream strain of cannabis, and a bit of mullein leaf I had picked and dried. I had formulated this blend because mullein is a medicinal herb that soothes and moistens the lungs and produces a cool, fluffy smoke, while passionflower is a nervine, an anti-anxiety herb that helps us open the heart and assists with receiving spiritual insight. Sometimes I added some dried lavender flowers to the blend, as well, to add a mild menthol effect and aroma.

I turned off the lights and lit vanilla candles, and misted rose and lilac water in the air.

Once we had smoked ourselves into a sufficiently altered state, I turned off the music and lit a bundle of dried Western Red Cedar leaves that I'd gathered to bless the space with protective energy. I waved the smoke through the room with a fan I had made of hawk feathers plucked from roadkill birds.

We sat cross-legged on the floor in a circle in a special section of my apartment that I had blessed with vibrant streams of Reiki energy.

These events consistently produced visions for all involved. One time in particular was especially potent.

"This is a tincture of a lichen, which is a combination of an algae and fungus. It's called Usnea, and is colloquially known as Old Man's Beard. It grows on the tree branches in old growth forests. It is used as an herbal medicine for pneumonia and bronchitis," I told the group.

I passed around an amber glass bottle containing the extract I had made so each person could take a moment to bring the medicine to their heart with gratitude and imbue it with love. Then we passed it around again and placed a dropperful of the tincture in our mouths so that we could connect with the physical energy of the plant. And then we sat in silence for about twenty minutes.

I felt swirling masses of energy tingling around me and then I had a closed-eye vision of a tipi. Inside the tipi I saw a baby crawling on a round red rug. Outside the tipi there was a Sioux warrior-shaman-chief wearing a headdress with eagle feathers. He could see me and we were telepathically linked; he was sending a stream of energetic activations from his third eye to my own in a sort of transdimensional mind-meld. Stranger still, I had the distinct awareness that I was actually looking at myself in a past life, that *he* was *me*.

While this was happening, I heard the sound of women whispering in my ear repetitively. Their voices kept saying, "Get a drum. Get a drum. Get a drum. Get a drum. Get a drum."

When the vision subsided, I opened my eyes and shared my experience with my friends. I was amazed to find out that the two people sitting on either side of me said that they had heard the spirits audibly whispering to me, too!

I did get a drum after that. I arranged to meet a drum maker named Michelle Meiser, the owner of Gaia's Workshop, and she showed me a beautiful horsehide drum with an uncanny resemblance to a full moon. She even knew the life story of the animal it had come from. I knew it was the one. It was perfect. A seamstress friend made me a lovely hand-sown carrying case for it, as well.

After many mystical experiences with the Moon Tribe, I wanted to share ganja as a spirit medicine with the public in the way it deserves to be understood: as a sacred herb worthy of respect. I organized my first public cannabis ceremony at Flanders House, an event space used for spiritual workshops in Portland, Oregon, and spread the word about it through social media. Some thirty people showed up. I had brought two strains, both from organic, outdoor herbs grown by yogi farmers. One strain was very high in CBD – cannabidiol, the soothing, pain-relieving, anxiety-reducing compound – and fairly low in THC – the active ingredient that makes you feel high, and the other one was the opposite, very high in THC, which stands for delta-9-tetrahydrocannabinol. I encouraged the participants to smoke whichever they felt most comfortable ingesting. That way, newbies and sensitive types could take it easy while the heavier users could go deeper and feel more of an effect. I wanted us all to be on a similar wavelength, and I felt that having two plants grown in the same place – by yogi growers, at that – would do it.

We burned sage and palo santo to cleanse our auras, and then we gave thanks to cannabis as a spirit teacher and smoked ganja together outside. Then we went inside to the ceremony space for a guided meditation that I led. I infused the group with Reiki energy blessings and did a little bit of shamanic drumming as well. I had encouraged people to bring their own instruments and at the end of the ceremony we had a collective jam session, which was great fun – everyone was on the same frequency and so we created harmonious music together. Afterwards, there was a potluck of tea and snacks and people hung around to discuss the experience, which for many participants had been quite powerful. Some broke into tears as they recounted having major life-changing realizations during the meditation. Many said they had gone extremely deep into trance. Others said it had been a profound experience just to smoke cannabis in an intentional way with like-minded strangers. I was glad we did it.

But the most memorable thing about the ceremony for me was actually something that happened right before it began. When I was on my way to set up the ceremony space, as I approached the entrance to the building, I saw a group of Tibetan Buddhist monks in traditional orange and ochre robes walking up the stairs in front of me, heading to the second floor.

I was intrigued by this unusual sight, so I followed them to find out what they were doing. They did not speak English so I was referred to their translator. I introduced myself and asked him what was going on.

"A Green Tara Empowerment Ceremony," he said.

"How interesting," I said. "I'm going to be leading a cannabis ceremony right below you in just a few minutes. I was planning to do some drumming. I hope that won't disturb your ceremony. Is it going to interfere?"

When the translator relayed my question to the Tibetans, the monks all started laughing.

"Drum is good!" he said. "Drum is Tara noise!"

I didn't get the joke. What was so funny? I supposed Tibetan Buddhist monks would probably be zen and lighthearted about things, the type of people to gracefully embrace whatever happened, so I interpreted their laughter as an indication that life itself was just funny at that level of enlightenment.

But seven years later, I was doing a little background research for this book and I happened to find an article on the origins of Green Tara written by Lama Zoma Rinpoche that gave me a new perspective on this exchange. Now I get the joke.

"The venerable Tara, a female aspect of the Buddha, was originally born as a princess called Yeshe Dawa in the world called Manifold Lights. She was greatly devoted to the teachings of the buddha of that period whose name was Drum Sound, and for many hundreds of millions of years made offerings to the numberless buddhas, bodhisattvas, and arhats of the time. Each day she would prepare offerings of precious cloth in each of the ten directions, and because of the merits of this, she received bodhichitta…

Remaining in the palace, unattached to the sense objects she enjoyed, she practiced meditation and attained the state known as 'Releasing All Living Beings.'

Through the power of this, each and every morning she released hundreds of millions of others from worldly thoughts, bringing them to the same level, and every afternoon she did the same. Then she changed her name to 'Tara' – the Liberator – and consequently, the buddha Drum Sound prophesied that she would be known as the Goddess Tara until all sentient beings received enlightenment."[1]

A drum sound is a Tara noise, indeed!

---

[1] The essay continues, "In Tibet, countless Tibetan lamas have accomplished all the sutra and tantra realizations by relying on Tara. Among these are: Dromtonpa; Lama Tsong Khapa; the great yogi Landol Rinpoche; the great yogi who attained Arya Tara, Taguwa; the great teacher Yeshe Gyatso; the Venerable Ngawang Tsultrim; the Venerable Deupa Gyaltsen; the great Lama Jampa Tenzin Gyatso; the venerable lama, embodiment of all buddhas and manifestations of Tara herself in a human body, Losang Yeshe Tenzin Gyatso; the venerable, depthlessly kind Lama Lobsang Tsondu, who understands completely every single teaching of the Buddha and is the second buddha of wisdom, Manjushri; and innumerable others. Therefore, as long as we continue to observe the law of karma, we need never doubt that Tara will help us also to reach enlightenment."

7

EGO DEATH

When recreational cannabis became legal in Oregon, the industry celebrated with all-you-can-toke parties, fetes flooded with heaps of joints and dab rigs loaded with the most potent resin. These high-dose methods had effects sometimes bordering on the psychedelic.

It was at one of these parties that my friend Trina pulled me aside and said, "Tara, I'm afraid I'm going insane."

"Why?" I asked.

"Because I'm seeing colors around people," Trina said.

"You're not crazy at all. That's actually very good!" I told her.

"It is?" she asked.

"Yes! You're seeing colors because your third eye is opening, and your clairvoyance is awakening. People don't realize that cannabis stimulates the rise of kundalini energy in the spine," I said.

I knew this from direct experience. The process can be frightening or even traumatic if the person it is happening to has no framework with which to make sense of things.

One evening at home, my unassuming self took a few gentle puffs from a vape pen and settled into a hot epsom salt bath, expecting to unwind. Yet instead of relaxing, a terrible anxiety arose within me, grabbed hold of my psyche and would not let go. It began as a mild unease in the heart and spiraled into an intense, overwhelming sense of doom, which was not helped any by a powerful premonition that I was about to die.

Fortunately, I had a context in which to place this experience, because I had recently begun to study kriya yoga, the Indian tradition popularized by the master teacher Paramahamsa Yogananda in his book *Autobiography of a Yogi*. For this reason I had an awareness of the concept of kundalini awakening, and I knew that it often comes along with ego death. The yogis teach that kundalini normally is inert and latent at the base of the spine, until a kundalini awakening happens. The kundalini awakening is a metaphysical process in which a powerful surge of high-frequency, divine energy suddenly shoots up the spine, causing a profound spiritual activation. The consciousness expands into a great sense of oneness with the Universe, but first a person's psyche can feel as though it is being broken apart and obliterated. Thus the smaller, more limited identity, or self-concept known as the "ego", can experience kundalini awakening as death, psychologically.

I figured that this was probably what was happening to me, and that the feeling of overwhelming impending doom I sensed was only the fearful ego's perception of death, but even with this awareness, it was still quite emotionally harrowing to experience. There was some comfort in discovering that there was very much a physical process underway: When I tried to stand up to get out of the tub, I felt so dangerously dizzy that I immediately sat back down. I tried a few more times and had the same result. This told me that there really was something happening to me, and I suspected that it was due to an influx of high-frequency electromagnetic energy that my nervous system had not yet integrated. I waited for the light-headedness to abate enough for me to move safely, and then I gathered my towel around me and made my way to my bedroom, where I had a meditation space.

Although my meditation space was very peaceful and quiet, the input on my senses from the physical world felt unbearably overwhelming, even nauseating. I found the only way to fully tune it out was to lay face down on the soft carpet, and so that's what I did, crawling from my meditation cushion to the floor very slowly. Some part of me observing all of this felt very silly indeed, but here I was, and there was nothing to do but accept it. I sent up a silent prayer for my safety. Once the physical world had been removed from my awareness, vivid sounds appeared. In my left ear, I heard lovely, melodic wooden flutes. Simultaneously, in my right ear, thumping electronic dance music played. Intuitively, I knew this strange experience was a shamanic activation of sound waves coming from another realm or dimension. It seemed to go on for a long time. I have no way to judge the exact duration, but it seemed to last something like twenty minutes.

Eventually the music stopped and I gradually returned awareness to my body. When I peeled myself off the ground I felt completely normal again, able to make sense of things.

I was surprised that something very similar happened to me once again a short time later – and also involving cannabis, and also in the bathroom, for some reason. That second time, it was at night and I couldn't sleep, so I took just a few hits of cannabis from a glass pipe to try to relax, and then I got up from the bed and went to go pee. But as soon as I crossed the threshold to the tile floor, I felt something happening. A profound blackness fell over my eyes, rendering my vision inert. Then my legs were suddenly immobilized, feeling as though they had been glued to the floor with cement. I felt nauseous, and also there was that familiar feeling of doom again. Meanwhile, there was a very loud buzzing noise and a vibrating sensation in my brain. It sounded and felt as if it were electronic and mechanical, like things were physically shifting. I knew I could do nothing except wait it out. Once I could use my eyes and walk again, I went back to bed, where I lay awake the rest of the night recovering. It was all very startling and strange, but I emerged in the morning unscathed, aware that I had just received another energetic activation.

My heart goes out to the many people who have likely had similar experiences with cannabis and had no idea what was happening.

This is why I began to give public lectures on the use of cannabis as a tool for spiritual development. When imbibed with intention, ganja can do so much more than just make us feel relaxed and giggly. It can catapult our spiritual development, whether we feel ready or not.

When I gave these talks, people in the audience often expressed relief, raising their hands to say that they had long hidden their own enthusiasm for weed from friends and colleagues, even carrying a sense of guilt about it because so many of the spiritual communities they are part of still misunderstand it and demonize weed as "unclean" and "low-vibrational" – including, oddly, many yogic and ayahuasca groups, which sometimes parrot negative judgments about cannabis as "impure," or polluting the physical body. This unfortunate misunderstanding has permeated even the plant-medicine world, ironically. Most of the well-known American herbalist training programs I know of actually left cannabis out of the curriculum until very recently, despite the fact that it has a long history of use as an herbal remedy!

Once I even heard a rumor myself from friends in the ayahuasca circles I attended that *Madre* doesn't like cannabis and doesn't want people to use it. This sounded unlikely to me, especially because I had read about groups in Central America that combine the two plants together in their ceremonies. Still, I was open minded and curious to find out for myself if it was true. I decided to go directly to the source and ask *Madre* Ayahuasca herself what she thinks about cannabis. Her response? She told me she calls cannabis "Little Sister." That sounds like a warm embrace to me.

8

CANNABIS REIKI

I have often chosen to commune with ganja at times when I felt like a mystery to myself, and She revealed to me my innermost workings, thoughts and feelings that I had forgotten, avoided or repressed, guiding me to face myself with great gentleness.

This is why I began to incorporate ganja into my work as a spiritual counselor and Reiki healer: I noticed that when done with intention, hitting the bong gave my clients a heightened intuitive awareness, and amplified inner truths so that they could know themselves better.

Of course, cannabis is not an ideal medicine for everybody. There are those unsuited to it. Because it stimulates the opening of the upper chakras, cannabis can be quite ungrounding. People who are kind of spacy and not connected to the present moment tend to find that ganja just makes them more scatterbrained, which is really not helpful. And because it directs the gaze inward, cannabis can also potentially make an already introspective person excessively navel-gazing if overused. Additionally, people who are not psychologically balanced can find that cannabis exacerbates their problems. It can open the auric field too much. This medicine is best for a grounded, present individual who is generally psychologically stable and could really just use some help to open up, look within, and see things from a higher perspective – pardon the pun.

When a man named Gato came to see me about chronic pain, I sensed he would be an excellent fit for this approach.

"Tara, do you think your herbs can help me?" he asked. "My neck hurts, and I don't want to take painkillers."

"Sure," I said. "Let's do a cannabis Reiki session."

Gato, a handsome man in his thirties with a charming Mexican accent, had rarely ever smoked weed in his life. It just wasn't his thing. But he was open-minded enough to try it as a medicine, in the context of a healing ceremony.

After we set an intention together for his healing, I used a special wooden pipe called a *tepi* to blow a pea-sized amount of hapé tobacco medicine up his nostrils in order to ground him and anchor his consciousness into the Earth. Next, I handed him a purple glass bong packed with ganja, which happened to be a White Widow strain. He flicked a lighter and took a couple of big rips and coughed. As the medicine took effect, I asked him to notice what was different. He remarked that he was now experiencing a heightened sense of awareness.

I guided him to use this altered state to deeply examine the stuck energy in his neck that was manifesting as pain. "What is the texture of the energy?" I asked. "What does it feel like? What is it made of?" When he sensed into it very deeply, he recognized for the first time that it was actually a buildup of sadness. The ganja helped him to go even deeper than that, though.

He had an epiphany that he had been suppressing sadness throughout his life, and that this is where it had compounded, settling in his neck and condensing until it hurt physically. Like many men, as a boy he had been raised to believe that crying is a weak and un-masculine thing to do, so he had not allowed himself to do it.

"Crying is a physical process by which the body is able to release the energy of pain. It's very healthy and natural for people to cry. We need to cry. And crying is not weakness," I said. "It actually takes a very strong person to be willing to feel pain, and to express it is vulnerable. Crying takes courage, the courage to feel."

"I want to, but I can't do it," Gato said.

All of that conditioning had left him too repressed.

"No problem," I said. "You will. We just need some divine intervention. I can use Reiki to clear away the old conditioning stuck in your neural network. Would you like that?"

"Yes," Gato said.

Reiki is a special frequency of high vibrational divine energy that brings miraculous shifts for the better wherever it is directed, through intention, by an initiated healer. It removes blockages, and in places where there was once pain, it leaves serenity. It is a quantum medicine that works outside of space and time and can be sent to the past as well as the present. It works on the physical body, the emotions, and the spirit all at once because everything is fundamentally a form of energy; the variation between these things is only density. And it does not require touch. That is why I was able to share Reiki with Gato while seated across from him. All I needed was his consent.

As Reiki flowed into Gato's psyche, tears were forming at the edges of his eyes. They streamed down his cheeks until he reached for a tissue to dab them. And then he sobbed, quietly at first, and then more and more fully.

"This is wonderful," I told him. "You're releasing blocked energy and healing yourself. Thank you for trusting me to witness this."

When he had finished, there was a pile of crumpled tissues at his lap.

"How does your neck feel now?" I asked him.

"It feels good," he said, moving his head from side to side and looking surprised. When he stood up and moved, he said that not only had his neck pain gone away, but his chronic knee pain had disappeared, too.

When I checked in with him weeks and months later, Gato said it had stayed that way.

I was thrilled for him, but not surprised, because I had seen this very same phenomenon before. Oftentimes, chronic pain is a manifestation of unresolved emotional trauma or blockage made of emotional suffering that has been suppressed.

One of my first Reiki clients was a grandmother who had been suffering severe knee pain so bad she could hardly walk. She had had multiple surgeries, and her doctors told her that she needed another one as soon as possible. Unfortunately, she had been given an insufficient dose of anesthesia during the previous surgeries and actually felt the knife working on her, which had been awfully traumatic. That is why she was hoping to find an alternative treatment. She lived in the Midwest and didn't have many options, so when she came to the West Coast to see her kids, she Googled "Reiki" and "Portland" and found me. It was her first time trying Reiki.

When she came to see me, she laid down on a massage table, and I sat across from her in a chair at her feet. Both of us had our eyes closed. I channeled Reiki and meanwhile, I asked her about her life. She talked for hours about how she had suffered in an abusive marriage. Her husband had been very cold and mean to her, and had neglected her for years. I listened with compassion, validated her feelings, and trusted the Reiki energy to flow and clear away all her emotional pain. When we were done, three hours had passed, she had cried many tears, and she said she felt much better and emotionally lighter.

When she stood up, she was amazed to discover that her knees didn't hurt anymore. She walked out of the room quite delighted that she could move with ease. She was really shocked, because she had hobbled in! Weeks later, she contacted me by e-mail to say that her doctors were mystified at her sudden recovery. They told her that she no longer needed surgery, and her cholesterol and blood pressure readings had dramatically improved, too. She was very grateful.

9

REIKI

The poet Rumi wrote, "The wound is the place where the Light gets in."

That was true for me. My introduction to the healing arts came by way of trauma.

I had just graduated college and was working at a daily newspaper as a copy editor, a night-shift job that got out at midnight and leant itself easily to hitting the party circuit right after, because you could stay out late, drink too much and sleep in as long as you wanted.

Well, there was one evening where I really overdid it. I was living with male roommates at the time, including one who was the son of a preacher. I had drunk myself into such a stupor that I couldn't move, and this guy saw it as an opportunity to pursue his own gratification. He removed my clothing and attempted to sexually assault me, except that the physical effects of the whiskey he had drank left him unable to follow through. Nonetheless, it was a grave violation of consent and he was well aware of that. He was a dorky, bearded, bespectacled kid who looked like a cross between a lumberjack and an ogre, and there was never any flirtation between us, or any indication that I would have been interested in him. We weren't even friends, and we didn't hang out. He knew that what he was doing was wrong. I recall hearing him mutter something about how he was "being evil."

I was not OK after that incident, in a way I had never been before. It felt like something in the core of my being was gone. I felt like a shell of myself. I felt fundamentally unsafe, especially in places where there were men around. When I went out in public, I felt on the verge of a panic attack. It was hard to function. My spirit was broken.

I knew I needed to get help. I suspected that I needed something called a "soul retrieval," a special kind of trauma healing that shamans know how to do. Shamanic healing was on my radar because of my studies. At Rutgers University my undergraduate major had been philosophy with a minor in anthropology, and in my anthropology courses I had learned about mystical, indigenous healing technologies, and I read books about shamanism, which appealed to me very strongly.

By searching the Internet, I found a woman healer in northern New Jersey who had trained very seriously with Quechua-speaking people high in the Andes of Peru, and so I went to see her. Her treatment space was the finished basement of a nice big house in a rural town. It was dimly lit with just streams of sunshine pouring through the windows, and her space smelled of burned sage and tobacco.

I didn't tell her anything about what had happened to me. We simply sat across from each other, crossed legged on the floor, in meditation, with our eyes closed. She was silent, but I felt her presence all around me, as if she were floating behind me, beside me, and even above me, instead of sitting across from me, and I felt these pleasant swirls of energy coursing through my body. She told me to stand up, and when I did, my feet felt like they had suddenly become lead, glued to the ground like cement, and energy flowed through me and into the Earth like I was a tree. When it was over, I felt great. I felt like myself again, totally normal, restored to factory settings. I felt like nothing bad had ever happened to me, and the memory of that night seemed so faint now that it was easy to forget it ever had. The panicky feeling that something was missing was totally gone, replaced with a sense of inner serenity and wholeness.

I was truly amazed at the efficacy of her work, and very grateful.

This shaman, whose name was Jodee, told me that I could become her apprentice if I wanted to do that. She saw something in me, but it was hard for me to believe at that time that I could possibly have the kind of psychic healing gifts that she did. I was very intrigued and honored by her offer, but I didn't feel ready for that journey. I knew that I was too wild a partier to be able to commit to anything where I had to show up consistently in the morning and focus at that age. She told me that was OK, and that the call to learn about shamanic healing would return and destiny would kick in in my thirties.

She was right. The year Reiki entered my life was 2012. I was thirty.

Reiki was the catalyst that sparked the beginning of my spiritual journey.

My first encounter with Reiki was serendipitous. I had gone to see a hypnotherapist because I had a terrible case of writer's block that had struck very close to a major deadline for my first book, *Dandelion Hunter*. He told me I was disconnected from my feelings and my inner child and that I needed to do some inner work with the Reiki energy healer and spiritual counselor next door. I was open to that.

I arrived at my first Reiki appointment to find a very sweet and ebullient young woman about my age named Jeanette Hieter. Jeanette has a bright smile, long curly red hair, and an aura filled with kindness. She was easy to talk to and easy to trust. She worked out of an aqua-colored room with a tasteful wall hanging of the

Buddha done in shimmering gold paint. She invited me to recline on her massage table, covered me with a soft blanket and then guided me to gently close my eyes.

She talked about the different colors of energy moving through my body as she hovered above me and channeled the Reiki energy. I did not see the colors myself. Mainly, I experienced Reiki as deeply peaceful, soothing and relaxing. It seemed subtle, because I had not yet awakened my intuitive gifts, but I noticed that I did indeed have an easier time writing after seeing Jeanette, and so I came back to see her regularly both for that reason and because I liked the restorative, stress-relieving properties of the Reiki treatments. I also felt comforted by Jeanette's caring, nurturing presence and her nonjudgmental attitude towards anything I shared with her. I had gotten very little of that sort of thing in my life until then, and so seeing her was like finding an oasis of loving kindness.

I got a deeper appreciation for what Reiki could do while going through a devastating breakup with my boyfriend at the time. We'd had a passionate on-and-off relationship with a powerful magnetism between us, and the ending was intensely painful. When I went to see Jeanette for energy work, she blew my mind by using Reiki like a laser beam to vaporize my grief and heartache. I left feeling serene. It was as dramatic a shift as that first shamanic healing I had received in my early twenties. I had no idea Reiki could do that. I was amazed and dazzled by the efficacy of this mystical technology, and so I asked Jeanette if she would teach me how to do it. To my delight, she said yes, and organized a workshop.

I learned that Reiki was developed in early Twentieth Century Japan by a man named Mikao Usui, a mystic and spiritual seeker who had studied Buddhism and Taoism. While some people think Reiki might be traced back to ancient Tibet, and others point to analogues in other places, insofar as it is a codified system of energy healing with a set of specific symbols and a particular frequency, Usui was the originator.

Usui encountered Reiki quite unexpectedly. After experiencing significant personal setbacks in his life as a businessman, he was attending a twenty-one day meditation retreat on Mount Kurama. While there, contemplating his life direction and communing with nature, he stood under a waterfall and was miraculously graced with a new and sudden ability to channel divine healing energy. He discovered this accidentally: He stubbed his toe on the hike back, and, while grasping it, felt energy flow out his hands and relieve his pain. He was surprised and delighted.

Usui called this gift Reiki, "*Rei*" meaning universal and divine, and "*ki*" meaning energy. He explored its capabilities, and then created a system embedded with kanji-based symbols for teaching it and transmitting it to other people so that he could share it with the world and bring healing to others. One of his students was a Navy doctor named Chujiro Hayashi who ran clinics to help people and developed a set of protocols for physical healing. Dr. Hayashi trained one of his clients, a Hawaiian resident named Hawayo Takata, and she brought Reiki to America, originally teaching via oral transmission only. Her students wrote down the teachings and now there are multiple lineages stemming from them, including my own teacher's teachers.

At the workshop, Jeanette explained that the ability to transmit the specific frequency of healing energy that is Reiki comes via "attunements," which are formal initiations in which a master teacher activates the energy field of a student and passes on spiritual gifts. It's a little bit similar to what the yogic tradition calls "*shaktipat*," except it has a specific protocol that involves activating each chakra, connecting the student to the frequencies of their own Higher Self, and to the ancestral masters of Reiki.

There are multiple levels of initiations in Usui Reiki. The first level enables you to heal yourself, the second gives you the power to be a conduit to heal others, and the third makes you a Reiki master, empowering you to ignite the healing light within others and pass it on. I remember I told Jeanette very sincerely, "I am not going to be a healer. I just want to know how to heal myself." I really believed that, too!

While many teachers offer all three levels as a weekend workshop, Jeanette teaches them one at a time and goes in depth, insisting that her students take months to let the power of each level sink in, and to take time to integrate the shifts that the initiations bring. I'm glad she did.

Her Reiki Level One training brought me the desire to meditate and it came very easily to me, as if I was remembering something I already knew how to do and was very good at, instead of something unfamiliar and brand new. And I loved channeling the Reiki energy. I used it to relieve menstrual cramps, to relax before going to sleep, and to bless situations, loved ones, and the world. It was very empowering!

I also had the surprising urge to practice Reiki on my friends, which was something I hadn't expected to want to do. I was completely amazed to discover that as I did, I was getting intuitive messages and images that seemed random to me but that, when I shared them, turned out to be highly relevant to those I was practicing on. This was exciting and encouraging to me, because I had never really thought of myself as particularly intuitive before. Now I felt very eager to learn Level Two.

After that Level Two initiation and training, a door opened for me to become the intuitive healer in residence at a local wellness center that had regular Friday night social events for the community, and I loved it. I got to see Reiki work real miracles. Grieving people found that just one hour of receiving Reiki was enough to take away the pain in their hearts, replacing it with love and peace, just as I myself had experienced. There was a woman who came to see me hoping to find relief for her PTSD symptoms, especially insomnia, and after one treatment she reported a total shift into a greater sense of inner peace and a good night's sleep. The more I did Reiki, the more amazed I was by it. Every time I did a session, amazing things happened.

I attracted students and clients effortlessly. People approached me and asked for help in all sorts of places – at the gas station, in cafes, in line at the drugstore – saying that they didn't know why, but they felt drawn to me for some reason. I had to get used to strangers walking up to me and immediately opening up and telling me heavy stories about their lives and what they were going through, as if there were a blinking neon sign over my head that everyone could see except me, saying, "Bare your troubles here." I believe it happened because spirit medicines have a way of magnetizing those who need them.

For instance, I was at an afternoon potluck garden party when a tall, lanky man in his mid-fifties approached me. He had curly gray hair and kind, smiling eyes. "I don't know what it is that you do," he said, "but my intuition is telling me that you're very good at it. Maybe you can help me."

He stood with his shoulders hunched over, as if his burdens were literally weighing on him and he was wrapped up in a blanket of shame and hurt. I wondered why.

When he came to see me for Reiki, I got a chance to find out. Healing energy flowed out of my hands with a subtle tingle and heat and I scanned the air above his body with my hands, looking for places where I felt pressure, heat or cold, or tingling. I found such a place above his abdomen. As I hovered there, he began to weep. I brought him a box of tissues, and continued hovering above him.

Psychically, the spot on his abdomen began to appear to me like an infected wound, and then a vision came to me. I felt a story arise inside my body, and an internal nudge to open my mouth to share it.

"I am seeing that you had a lifetime where you were a Native American man," I told him. "I don't know what tribe it was. In this lifetime, you were someone with some amount of authority and status, perhaps a chief, or a warrior, something like that. There was a massacre, and in your absence, the women and children were killed. Your family was murdered. You blamed yourself for not defending them."

He sobbed and took deep, painful breaths.

I felt the ghosts of his slain family standing there around us in the room. I felt they had come to help, because they loved him. "They forgive you, and they want you to forgive yourself," I told him.

I felt chills and got goosebumps as I said these words, and he sobbed deeply as Reiki flowed through me to help him release himself from blame.

After that session, he was a changed man. He even looked different. He stood taller and there was a lightness in his face. The heaviness he had carried before was gone. He called me several times in the following weeks to express his gratitude.

But of course, it wasn't my doing. Reiki is by definition divinely guided energy. Unlike some other forms of energy healing, Reiki requires its practitioners to be conduits more than active facilitators. A skilled Reiki healer embodies non-effort, non-striving, and just being. As a friend of mine once said, "You're very good at getting out of the way." Doing it well amounts to being a passive witness and a loving presence, while holding great trust in your heart and empowering the ceremony of healing with your intention.

The more I let go, the more amazing things became. There was a woman who came to me wanting to heal childhood trauma to do with sexual abuse. I sent Reiki to her past (which, as a quantum technology, Reiki can do), and as the healing light flowed, I received a vision. I saw a queen with a golden crown casting a curse upon the ancestors of my client. The purpose of the curse, I sensed, was to rob them of their innocence, and thus, their magical power.

When I shared this vision with her, she told me that she already knew about it! She said her grandmother had told her that in centuries past, the Queen of England had placed a curse upon her family in Ireland! I sent Reiki healing to the souls of all of her ancestors who had suffered in this way and prayed to end the curse, and both of us felt an energy shift as divine intervention was granted and peace and love flowed into her body and beyond.

On Earth we humans exist in lower densities of vibrational energy than exists in the realm of Heaven. Thus we need intermediaries to act as bridges and "step down" the high frequency divine healing energy into a physical human body so that others can access it. Initiated healers are like transistors, or electrical transfer stations, in that way.

The initiation process that turns a person into a Reiki healer, the "attunements," make changes in the nervous system so that we can receive and transmit these frequencies of Heavenly light through our physical body. We go through a recalibration process that can be physically exhausting and emotionally challenging. The attunement process often prompts involuntary physical detoxing that occurs when you get connected to greater amounts of light, which to me felt like having a hangover or a mild flu for several days to a week or more. Each person's system does what it needs to do in order to make room.

The more attunements a healer receives, the more psychic she becomes, and the more potent the healing energy is that she can hold, radiate and channel, because a larger bandwidth becomes available. When I became a Reiki master, I discovered that every time I initiated a new healer, I went through the detox process again. And this was a good thing, because the more heavy energies you release, the clearer a vessel you become.

In my case, there was a tremendous amount of material to process and clear out as I integrated the attunements. I had a lot of wounds to unravel and much recovery to do, especially when it came time to heal from my childhood, which was a period of great unhappiness and suffering for me. At school there was bullying. At home there was abuse.

It's not easy to write that word, "abuse," because my parents are also honest, well-intentioned people who did their very best to give me a good life. They took me to Disney World. They showed up at my sports games to cheer me on. They celebrated my birthdays with cake and presents. They sent me to summer camp. They bought me a Ford Mustang when I turned eighteen, and they paid for college. They cared about me, and genuinely meant well.

Yet they were also flawed human beings like the rest of us, and I don't know what else to call it when your father hits you in rage and says awful, scarring things about how you are a worthless human being – frequently, starting when you are a little girl, and continuing until you're a teenager big enough to fight back. And I don't know what else to call it when you come home crying from school and your mother rolls her eyes at your tears and coldly mocks you, saying, "Oh boo-hoo" – and blames you, saying you probably deserved it. After all, she resents you for being the reason her husband exposes his monstrous side, and so her heart is calloused towards your pain.

I stood up to my father all the time. Mom preferred to swallow her words and walk on eggshells around him. She didn't understand why I refused to do the same. She used to say, "Do you want to be right or do you want to be happy?"

I wanted to be happy, but self-betrayal was too high a price to pay, so I talked back, come what may. And sometimes what came was explosive.

For instance, Dad would say, "You're supposed to respect me because I'm your father."

And I would reply, "If you want my respect, then you have to act in ways that are worthy of it."

He would exclaim, exasperated, "You're making me angry!"

"I can't *make you* feel or *do* anything," I answered. "You're an adult. Act like one." I think I was about nine when I said that.

Sometimes Dad and I just argued bitterly until one of us stormed off and other times, in my teenage years, Dad chased me around the house yelling at me, and when he caught me he'd pin my wrists to the wall and spit in my face, saying the meanest and most damaging things he could think of, while dodging the fruitless kicks I tried to launch at him. He was much, much bigger than me, six feet two and nearly three hundred pounds. He mostly found my attempts to fight back rather humorous.

If I had not had exercise as an outlet, or the deep love of the family dog to comfort me through those difficult times, I think I might have succumbed to the feelings of hopelessness and despair that sometimes left me contemplating a premature exit. But I knew that life would get much better when I left for college. It was like a prison sentence with a release date. In the meantime I coped by disconnecting from my emotions so that I could shut out the pain I felt. I took the dog jogging, went for long walks in nature with my friends, threw myself into my schoolwork, and played on sports teams. And when something bad happened at home, I'd write it down in my diary and then I'd rip out the pages and throw them away, so I could pretend it had never happened.

Abuse is a generational plague, and today I do forgive my parents, because I recognize that they too were suffering its effects, the twisted inheritance of dysfunction. Their ugliest behavior does not define them in my mind, just as I don't define myself by my own worst moments. (As my spirit teachers once said to me, "The behavior is not the person.") Now that I am grown, Dad has since apologized to me with many tears of sincere remorse, saying that he wishes he could go back in time and do things differently. Sometimes he apologized when I was a child, too. But that didn't change the damage it did.

It took many well-spent years in Twelve Step rooms and at least a thousand sessions with Jeanette to unravel all of that. My being a sane and healthy adult today is very much a testament to the healing power of spiritual remedies. I am deeply grateful to Reiki, and to Jeanette's incredible skills as a psychic counselor. Jeanette was able to perceive the subconscious thoughts, beliefs, and emotions that I had once kept hidden from myself, and with her gentle assistance, I was able to face them, feel them, and release them.

I invested everything I could in my recovery. I pursued it with a burning fire of determination, because I understood that to do so was not just to gain peace and wholeness inside myself, but that it was also the very curriculum of my apprenticeship as a healer. There were periods when I was booking three healings a week with Jeanette and other gifted practitioners. As I worked to overcome my childhood trauma, anxiety and depression, self-esteem problems, dysfunctional relationships, and many kinds of neuroses, I knew that many, many people were facing the very same obstacles, and I realized that I was gaining the tools to help them, too. I became fearless about witnessing the depths of other people's suffering as a healer, because I had already gone there inside myself. I was filled with empathy.

As my career as a teacher and healer progressed, I taught Reiki to others and I led workshops at metaphysical stores on self-love, finding your purpose, and plant spirit medicine. Eventually I felt a calling to start training apprentices formally, so I organized nine-month group courses. But as I took steps to publicize my work, I began to experience a very intense, overwhelming anxiety.

I didn't doubt my abilities, yet I felt major fear about putting myself out there that went way beyond normal jitters. It triggered something irrational within me that reacted as if going more public was somehow very, very dangerous. It was strange because there wasn't any particular experience that I was aware of in my past that I could connect to these feelings. I did not know the root of it, and I needed to find the root of it in order to dig it up and plant something better.

Though I usually worked with Jeanette, this time I felt guided to enlist the services of Laural Virtues Wauters, who is a shamanic healer, Reiki master, author, former professional therapist and teacher trained by the Four Winds Society. Laural worked over the phone, as many healers do, and as I do now myself. Laural did indeed locate the root of my fears, and it was nothing at all like I expected.

I will never forget what she told me.

After about ten minutes of melodic drumming that put her into a shamanic trance, Laural recounted an incredibly detailed vision.

"You were an African woman," she told me, "and very beautiful. And you were a powerful shaman for your tribe. This was unusual, because shamans were usually men, and usually older men. But you were gifted. There was a lot of jealousy, especially among the other women in your tribe. It was said that you had too much power. They started rumors and it got ugly. Some of those in your tribe who hated you conspired with a neighboring tribe who feared you to attack you. You had large breasts, and they thought that this was the source of your power, so they cut them off and left you for dead.

They thought that they had killed you, and you very nearly died, but a shaman from another tribe, an older man, secretly grabbed you under cover of night and nursed you back to health. He put plants on your chest and salves and you recovered. You could not go back to your tribe, because they would try to kill you again. So, you wore a chest-plate and lived in his tribe as a man. You continued your shamanic work there, and meanwhile you had an affair with the healer's son, a man your age. This man got you pregnant, and once again, this tribe began to fear you. They thought you had too much power, because you were a man who was able to become pregnant. When you gave birth, some in the tribe believed your baby was a demon, and so you had to flee. Both you and your child were at risk of being killed," she said.

"You went out into the desert and found a herd of elephants. They were matriarchal and telepathic, and they took you in and protected you. You helped them, healing them with herbs, and your child, a son, became very good at finding water. You lived with them, wandering the desert, for twelve years, and then you died. One of the elephants was so heartbroken that it, too, died on your grave. Your son eventually became part of a village, where he was celebrated for his talents as a douser. He is now one of your spirit guides, and takes the form of a bat. He helps you to sense energy."

I felt extremely tired after that healing, and I slept very deeply for twelve hours, three days in a row. I noticed a change inside my heart as well: instead of hesitancy and apprehension, I felt courage and confidence when I thought about teaching my apprentices, and I was able to move forward with it.

It is fascinating to consider how complex our psyches really are, and how we can be deeply affected in this lifetime by experiences that actually predate our own birth. Fortunately, skilled healers like Laural can liberate us to evolve beyond them.

Since then, I have had the opportunity to learn about many more of my past lives through healing ceremonies. I was usually a shaman or an herbalist, but not always.

I have learned, for instance, about a lifetime in which I sacrificed my body to feed a hungry lion, as part of a spiritually guided initiation through dismemberment; a lifetime in which I was a child-bride in Southeast Asia; a lifetime as a slave; one as someone's pet bird with clipped wings. Once I was an Andean tribe woman murdered by a spurned suitor who pushed me off the edge of a cliff during a tribal dance and made it look like an accident. In the Middle Ages, I was an herbalist who lived by herself in the forest most of the time, but occasionally donned armor to disguise herself as a man and then fought on horseback in battles. In the pioneer days, I died on the Oregon Trail. In another life in early America, I was a white woman who left her culture to go live with the "Indians."

Apparently, I have had many adventures.

10

TOO MUCH GANJA

In theory, it isn't possible to overdose on ganja, at least not in a lethal way. According to the National Institute on Drug Abuse, no one has ever died from ingesting too much THC, the active ingredient in cannabis. It doesn't appear to be possible, perhaps because cannabinoids are endogenous to the human body.

As humans, we are very literally wired for cannabis.

According to Peter Grinspoon, MD, in an article for Harvard Medical School's *Harvard Health Publishing*: "The 'cannabinoid' receptors in the brain — the CB1 receptors — outnumber many of the other receptor types in the brain. They act like traffic cops to control the levels and activity of most of the other neurotransmitters. This is how they regulate things: by immediate feedback, turning up or down the activity of whichever system needs to be adjusted, whether that is hunger, temperature, or alertness. To stimulate these receptors, our bodies produce molecules called endocannabinoids, which have a structural similarity to molecules in the cannabis plant. The first endocannabinoid that was discovered was named anandamide after the Sanskrit word *ananda* for bliss. All of us have tiny cannabis-like molecules floating around in our brains."

Yet sometimes, people feel anxious about this medicine, and we can fear that we have taken too much of it.

When cannabis was newly legal in Oregon, some people who had never smoked before wanted to give it a try. One such person asked me to guide her through her first time. This woman was a fellow Reiki master, a single mother who wanted to experiment and do something adventurous in a safe way. She was very sensitive. She took a few hits from a cannabis pipe, and then as soon as she put the pipe down, she started to worry.

"I think I smoked too much," she said.

"'Too much' is a judgment. What you really mean is that you smoked more than you're comfortable with, and now you feel vulnerable," I replied.

"Yes, that's it," she said.

"You are safe," I told her. "It is pretty much impossible to overdose."

I knew this not just because of science, but also from personal experience. I had about twenty-five years of getting really, really stoned behind me. And in this time I had ingested copious amounts of THC, especially this one particular time when I happened to be working on a pot farm near Garberville, California, in Humboldt County, a place that was the unofficial capital of weed growing back when it was only available on the black market.

I had a very tedious job as a "trimmer" there, which required great focus and concentration to clip the leaves off dried ganja buds with tiny scissors for twelve hours a day every day. I lasted a week at this grueling labor. My hands got so sore. I did it because it paid cash under the table. Back then, cannabis was still illegal. The work crew was an eclectic mix of people, myself and five or six Israelis who were traveling through, two of whom were friends of mine (I knew one woman named Bar from Portland, and the other I had met there). Everyone was speaking Hebrew except for me, and we were all toiling away inside a tiny, rustic two-room homestead that was more or less an old barn.

Given that I was needing to sit still for very long stretches and had no one to talk to, I wanted to get as stoned as I could. Thus, I decided to bake pot brownies for everybody, and an old hippie with some teeth missing named Susie, who was one of the farmers of this homestead, pointed to a paper plate filled with a mountain of powdery kief – crystallized cannabis resin – to put in them and said, "Use as much as you want." I had never used kief before and was totally unfamiliar with the potency of this substance – which, it should be noted, is highly concentrated.

Winging it, I poured it all in and therefore stirred two heaping cups of kief into this batter to make one tray of brownies. I did not realize that that was an insane dose of THC. It probably amounted to something like 200 mg of THC per brownie, maybe more. For comparison, most store-bought cannabis edible products have 5 to 10 mg of THC per serving. But we were out in the sticks in a place too remote to use a cell phone or get internet access, so I truly had no idea what I had just done. I just thought I was making run-of-the-mill pot brownies.

When I pulled the tray out of the oven and sliced them up, it did smell pretty pungent. I ate a couple pieces and then handed the rest out to the other trimmers and to Susie, the farmer. Susie took just one bite and looked at me like I was crazy.

"Girl, you're trying to send me to the moon!" she exclaimed. "I'm not taking another bite!"

Only then did I start to suspect I was in for more than I had expected, but I wasn't worried. I thought I was a canna-pro, so I just sat down on the couch next to my friends and went back to trimming dried little leaves off the ganja buds with little nail scissors. But then came a sensation that felt like my stomach was being squeezed to death by an anaconda. I said to my friend Bar sitting next to me, "I'm not doing so well."

"Let's go sit outside and get some fresh air," Bar said. We linked arms and she helped me walk outside the farmhouse to sit on the front steps. This was in the Sierra Nevada mountains, high elevation, not too far from Garberville, California, and we were surrounded by a pristine forest of old growth trees. The beauty of it all struck my heart with such force that I vomited.

Bar's friend Gingy – we called him that because he was a redhead (gingy as in "ginger") – patted my back reassuringly while I hung my head between my knees, still feeling quite sick. Gingy was a very zen person who meditated every morning and he said gently in his thick Israeli accent, "It's part of it. It's all part of it."

The next thing I remember is going to sleep. When I woke up, it was three days later.

One would suppose I must have gotten up to pee at some point, but if so, I have no memory of it.

When I emerged from the bed after three days of deep sleep, I heard farmer Susie say, "She's alive!" and everyone was laughing.

Bar told me that, during my long absence, the farmers had played their piano and everyone had a stoned sing-a-long together, including one of the Israeli trimmers who happened to be a hard-ass cop in her home country. She had annoyed everyone by going on long anti-drug tirades, bragging haughtily that she had never smoked weed and was only tagging along with her friends for the money. The cop had not realized that there was weed in the brownie she ate, because she'd never tasted weed before. She accidentally got high for the first time in her life, because I accidentally dosed her, and from what I heard, she had a lot of fun – so much fun that she mellowed out and hopped off her high horse, to everyone's relief.

11

A MOST UNIQUE FORM
OF COUNSELING

I once worked an unconventional gig that lives somewhere between joining the circus and tending bar, except that it gets far less respect from society. Some people would call it stripping, but I thought of it more like being a naked acrobat. I climbed up a two-story pole and hung upside down by my thighs, dancing straight through twelve-hour shifts. I certainly got incredible amounts of exercise while twirling brazenly around in my undies and sometimes in nothing at all, and I had many memorable experiences, too. For one thing, that was where I met my good friend Bar, the Israeli woman who invited me to the ganja adventure.

For another, I did a lot of counseling work beneath those neon lights.

Though at first I thought people came to the club for the novelty or to experience the transgressive ambiance, I soon learned that there was more to it. They felt lonely, and talking to dancers offered a sense of human connection, and it was especially fulfilling because the anonymity of the environment made them feel safe to be honest and vulnerable.

For instance, there was one particular regular customer – a middle-aged, balding guy with a paunch, as many of them are – who used to tip me in magic mushrooms as well as cash. The place was a dive, and we were sitting in a dimly lit private booth with a sheer curtain blocking us off from the view of the bar and its satellite tables. Rock music was playing loudly on the speakers. It might have been something by The Strokes, or it could have been Bon Jovi, because both were popular at the time. He was paying me to listen, to give him my undivided attention. I'll never forget our first meeting.

"I don't know what's wrong with me," he was saying. "I get overwhelmed by my emotions. I can look at anyone and just know things about them. I could do it right now in the club."

"That's because you're an empath," I told him.

"'Empath'? What the fuck does that mean?" he asked.

"What you're describing are the characteristics of an empath: a highly sensitive, intuitive person who is tuned into the emotions of others," I said. "That is what you are."

"No shit?" He said. "I cry easily, all the time. Look, I'm weeping right now," he said, as tears flowed down his cheeks. "I don't know what's wrong with me."

"There's nothing wrong with you, dude. You're an empath. You just need to ground yourself so you don't get so overwhelmed and take on other people's feelings," I explained.

When the DJ called me up to the stage, this man sat in the front row and announced proudly to the other patrons, "That's my therapist up there!"

They looked a bit puzzled. "Really?" someone asked.

"Best therapist I ever had," the guy insisted.

After my set, I went to get a drink of water at the bar. My customer joined me there, and he was weeping again. Actually, he had burst into tears. "But this is a strip club," he was saying. "I'm not supposed to have a spiritual awakening in a strip club!"

He was the first guy this happened to, but he wasn't the last.

Another dancer at that club, a lithe, blonde woman, pulled me aside one day and said, "You're reading energy, aren't you?"

"How did you know?" I asked.

"Oh, I've been watching you. I do it too," she said.

It is not as rare as one might think. I have met more than a few professional intuitive healers who moonlight as dancers, and I know of some who work as professional prostitutes as well. Perhaps we are the modern version of those temple priestesses of long-ago who once shared their sacred sexuality with the intention of divine service in the goddess temples of ancient Greece, Rome, and the Middle East. Some of these lived in devotion to Aphrodite, goddess of love.

I danced on and off for several years, initially because it helped to pay bills that being a freelance journalist couldn't cover. The very first place I did it was a rural club in upstate New York, a place frequented by farmers and soldiers. One entertainer there was a lifer, a lady named Victoria who was in her late sixties.

Victoria was tall and had a soft, full figure she adorned with bleach-fried Eighties hair and some missing teeth. She certainly stuck out in stark contrast to the much younger, fitter women in that club, but she didn't try to pretend she was anything other than she was. She embraced it, fully. She was very lighthearted, joyful, and she laughed a lot. And although when she stepped on stage some men got out of their seats and walked away, looking disgusted, plenty of others came forward and gazed upon her totally smitten, in awe, and seemed really into her, because she loved herself, and that's the ultimate aphrodisiac.

12

GANJA VISION

A crowded music festival is no place for a sensitive empath. I didn't realize that until it was too late and I was well inside the multi-day music festival known as the Oregon Country Fair, a popular summer event near Eugene. I felt both overwhelmed and terribly smushed, pressed like a sardine in a tin of people.

"Want to sit on my shoulders?" my friend Johnananda offered. (He has this nickname because he's a follower of the great kriya yogi and author Paramahamsa Yogananda). Johnananda is a very tall and stocky fellow, built like a Viking with a bushy red beard. He is a gentle giant with a charitable heart, someone I had met when I worked as a metaphysical teacher and intuitive healer at New Renaissance Bookshop in Portland, where he was a manager and meditation leader. We ran into each other at the fair, and now he was taking pity on me.

I accepted his offer and he ducked down so I could swing my legs over his shoulders and then he stood up and I got to ride high above the swarm of people like a princess on a litter. Together we enjoyed some ganja cookies and then he walked us over to see some band I had never heard of, which was probably folk or jam-bandish sounding, as most stuff there was. At this show we ran into a mutual friend, a fellow Reiki master we knew named RT. I dismounted while the two of them danced together.

The THC from that edible became quite strong so I sat down on the ground by myself. Overcome with the impulse to turn inward, I closed my eyes and went deep into a meditative state.

Promptly, a vision appeared. A symphony of rainbow patterns came towards me in layers and each was accompanied by an exquisitely lovely wave of divine bliss and peace. Yet each was also taken away. And when it was, it was replaced by something very different that was satisfying in a new way, which was heightened by its contrast with the experience that had preceded it. This stream of gifts took the form of abstract beauty that I could feel as well as see, and I sensed that my task was to let go as it happened, going deeper and deeper into a state of non-attachment instead of clinging to what I liked and hoping to make it last. I could feel the delight of the Creator in this dance. It felt as if He was playing a game with me, like a parent dangling toys above a baby's crib. Melting into this state of deep surrender was a dazzling experience, and the more I relaxed into it, the more gorgeous it all became.

When I opened my eyes, my friend RT was looking at me, smiling.

"I saw that," he said.

"You saw *what*?" I asked.

"You did a Buddha thing," he said, his eyes shining.

When your friends are telepathic, everything happens in public.

13

PRIDE

"Power in the head is arrogance. Power in the heart is love."
- Maestro

Sometimes, the most spiritual people can have the biggest egos. Early in my spiritual journey, I myself was a good illustration of that common irony. Back then I made the rookie mistake of identifying with my gifts and interpreting them, and the amazing mystical experiences I was having, as reflections of myself and my worth. The truth is that intelligence, intuition, courage, and whatever other good qualities I thought I possessed were really only ever resources on loan from Heaven, gifts given for the purpose of sharing in service. They are reflections of the Creator, not the created. But I was not always tuned into that fact.

Heaven doesn't like its servants to be prideful, and it finds ways to realign us when we get out of balance. It does so not to punish us, but rather to help us develop a healthy sense of humility where it is lacking. My first such lesson was a memorable one.

After a long winter of overcast skies and cold weather in Oregon, the wild roses were in bloom, hiking trails beckoned, and I looked forward to floating down the gentle currents of the Clackamas River in the summer, gazing at the rock walls and gorgeous hanging lianas.

Just before the solstice, I dropped in to a yoga class. And in that class, the teacher asked us to hold a difficult pose for five long minutes. When I walked out the door afterwards, my left knee didn't feel quite right. By the next morning, it had swelled massively. It really hurt.

I went to an urgent care center, and the doctor told me I had sprained my knee and would need to be on crutches for quite awhile, six weeks at least. This was upsetting, because it meant all those fun outdoor activities I had been looking forward to all winter were not going to happen. It meant I couldn't go on my morning jogs for a while, either.

I went out for a long walk down the urban street where I lived on my crutches, glad that I was at least still mobile.

"Trying out for the Olympics?" one stranger quipped.

"What happened?" a man demanded to know as I passed by. When I didn't respond, he cursed at me, angry that I hadn't divulged the details of my life.

I felt a heaviness in my upper back, a spreading sensation of embarrassment. As a person who had prided myself on being strong and athletic and independent, it was very uncomfortable to feel so fragile and vulnerable.

As I crossed paths with people who hobbled with canes or sat in wheelchairs, we exchanged empathetic glances. "You're one of us," their eyes seemed to say.

My situation quickly deteriorated. Perhaps because I had been so active, walking around and putting so much weight on the other leg, my *other* knee swelled up in pain. Then, my elbow got sprained. And then, my back seized up.

I was mostly bedridden at this point, hopped up on opiates and cannabis to manage the pain I was in. I lived alone, and could not take care of myself. I could not do basic things like carry groceries up the stairs to my apartment or do laundry or even carry a glass of water. Worst of all, I could not take care of my beloved dog either. I had to ask a friend to temporarily foster her until I recovered. And her absence made my situation even lonelier.

I crawled on the carpet to get to the bathroom, scooting myself around like a crab. There was a day when I could not get out of the bathtub. I felt so completely weak and helpless.

And there was a morning when I woke up and discovered to my horror that I was completely immobilized. Not only were my joints swollen and painful and rigid, the muscles in my back and neck had seized up so intensely that I couldn't turn to the right or left, not even a smidgen, without excruciating pain. I couldn't lift my head either. The panic I felt was terrible. I was completely unable to do this basic thing I had taken for granted a million times in the past: get out of bed. I had to go to the bathroom but I couldn't because my body was imprisoning me.

Slowly, painfully, I reached down and grabbed my cell phone with the one arm that wasn't messed up and texted a neighbor for help. He came over and saw me in my pajamas stuck in my bed, and though we barely knew each other, he graciously helped me get up.

I would love to say that this was the worst part, but it wasn't. In order to try and straighten my body out, I went to see a chiropractor. The chiropractor "adjusted" me by slamming my body violently into the treatment table. It was frightening and sharply painful. The trigger-point massage sessions I got were even worse, actually. As the therapist pressed into the knots throughout my body, I felt searing, excruciating pain. It was so awful I cried.

Things finally took a turn for the better when one of my plant medicine students, Corinne, took great pity on my sorrowful state and insisted I try acupuncture. She handed me a twenty-dollar bill and persuaded me to go to a community clinic she liked.

At the clinic, I sat in a recliner in a big, dim room with soothing music playing softly. It was filled with all sorts of people, some of whom were snoring. The acupuncturist stuck pins in my ears, the top of my head, in my hands and down my legs. This was surprisingly relaxing and I drifted off into a no-thought void, emerging after several hours, surprised to see the time because it felt like I had only sat there for ten minutes!

My body finally began to heal from the acupuncture, which I went to get almost daily.

One afternoon when I was doing better I stopped into a café. I had a little time before a physical therapy appointment. I stood in line there, hunched over my crutches, wobbling like an elderly person with a walker. I looked around for an open seat and all the tables were taken, and as I considered sitting outside, an older African American gentleman stood up and pointed to the seat at his table.

"You can sit here, and I'll get your tea for you," the man said.

I hesitated. I knew from experience that when a male stranger is generous towards me, it can come with ulterior motives revealed by a base hunger that shines out the eyes. But when I studied this man's face I saw only kind, soft eyes that registered my suffering and felt pained by it. This was a person who wanted to give, not take.

"I'm sorry you're hurt," he said.

"Thank you," I said. "That's really nice."

"I do one good deed a month," he said, grinning.

"Why?" I asked.

"Kindness. Everybody is struggling. Everybody is Sysiphus pushing the boulder up the mountain, and then watching it roll back down again," he said. "People don't want to show their struggles, but that's what ties us together and makes us human."

As we got to know each other, he shared that he was a professional speaker and author named Greg Bell.

"One day I was thinking about how I'd like to give a TED talk," Greg said. "It was just a passing thought. I barely even knew what a TED talk was. Then I went to a café, and I happened to help a man with something on his computer, and we got to talking just like this, and he told me he coordinated TED talks. And he asked me what I do, and I told him I'm the author of *Water the Bamboo*, and he looked it up and he said, 'That sounds interesting. You should give a TED talk.'"

"You gave a TED talk?" I asked.

"I did," he said.

"What is your book about?" I asked.

"Well, there's a kind of bamboo where if you water it for a year, two years, three years, nothing happens. And then suddenly, in 60 days, it shoots up."

Patience, I thought, seemed an apt theme.

At the physical therapist's office later, I asked how much longer I'd be hobbling around with two sprained knees.

"Have you ever watched a plant grow from a seed?" the therapist asked me.

"No," I said.

"The seed has to sprout and then the sprout has to grow roots and leaves. You can do things to make the soil conditions as conducive as possible, but it's going to take a certain amount of time to get there. I don't know what the amount of time is, but there is one, and doing more stuff doesn't make it happen faster."

(Again with the plant metaphors?)

As someone who was accustomed to exercising a couple hours a day most days, and for whom athleticism was a way of life, the ordeal felt interminable, but it wasn't. I was eventually able to walk without crutches again – at the very end of the summer.

14

THE CALL OF THE FROG

D eep in the Amazon rainforest, in the leafy branches of Peru, Brazil, Guiana and Colombia, there lives a species of big, lime-green tree frogs called *Phyllomedusa bicolor,* better known as kambo, sapo, or *dow-kiet.* These nocturnal amphibians crawl stealthily along arboreal appendages with fingers that wrap around the wood, munching on insects, and barking like dogs to call each other. When frightened or stressed, such as by snakes who sneak up on them and try to eat them, kambo frogs protect themselves by exuding a potent goo on their skin that stuns the predator and buys them time to escape.

People who live in the indigenous tribes there are known to climb trees and mimic their barking calls in order to capture these kambo frogs. Then they gently tie them up, scrape the goo off their bodies with sticks, and release them back to the jungle unharmed. They dry this goo into resin and wrap it in leaves, and then they carefully store it or they sell it to others for a fee, because this goo is prized – in the human body, it is a panacea.

The frog exudate is filled with medicinal compounds that are fungicidal, antiviral, antibacterial and immune boosting, plus it contains seven bioactive peptides: caeruelin, an analgesic; sauvagine, which acts on the pituitary and adrenal glands; phyllomedusin and phyllokinin, which dilate the blood vessels and increase permeability of the blood-brain barrier; and dermorphin and deltorphin, opioids that are nearly identical to the body's own natural pain-killers (beta-endorphins) and which are 18 to 39 times more potent than morphine, yet not addictive.

How do we know all of this? Because of ayahuasca.

There once lived an indigenous shaman named Kampu, and as the legend goes, he was the village healer for the Kaxinawa tribe in Brazil. His people were sick. Instead of the happiness and vibrance they were accustomed to, they were afflicted with the unusual symptoms of lethargy, depression and weakness. Kampu needed to find a remedy to help them, so he drank the sacred brew of ayahuasca. He knew this visionary tea would help him access divine guidance, and that in the ceremony, Spirit would teach him which of the many medicines in the Amazon jungle to use, and how to harvest and prepare it.

Ayahuasca showed Kampu that tree frogs held the cure. He was shown how to harvest medicine from the amphibians by scraping the goo off their skin with a stick and then applying it to the human body by first making small, superficial burns in the skin, which would send the frog exudate coursing through the lymphatic system and purifying it, removing toxins via emesis. Ayahuasca showed him that this medicine would restore the vitality of his people, healing their bodies as well as their spirits. It would clear away parasites and remove any negative energies that were weighing on them – including *panema,* funk that causes bad luck, as well.

Kampu dutifully followed the instructions he was given, and it worked. The frog medicine healed his people, cleansing their bodies and restoring their *joie de vivre.* Because the remedy worked so well, its use spread to other tribes, and it became known as *kambo,* in his honor.[2]

---

[2]   There may be other origin stories for kambo, legends and such, passed through oral tradition.

Kambo became more than just a curative medicine. The people who used it recognized the spiritual potency within it, especially its power for clearing the consciousness and raising your vibration, helping you to embody your soul, or Higher Self. This, combined with the physical discomfort of the process, is why kambo is now a component of warrior initiations and shamanic activations. And, because kambo reliably heightens both one's physical and metaphysical capacities, it is incorporated into pre-hunting rituals as well, because endurance and intuition are both highly useful assets worth sharpening ahead of long, difficult, multi-day tracking expeditions to capture animals in the bush.

Kambo came into my life quite unexpectedly. Though I enjoy studying ethnobotany and anthropology, I had never heard about it until an intuitive healer I knew, a fellow Reiki master with whom I rented a healing office, came back from a training program about it. This woman, who I'll call Kate, was very enthusiastic about kambo. She had just gotten a certification to facilitate treatments with it, and she was eager to use it.

"Kambo would be perfect for you," she told me. "You need it."

"Why?" I asked.

"It aligns you with your Higher Self, and it's great for times of transition," she said.

I was indeed in a transition. While I loved teaching herbalism because it empowered people to heal themselves with plants, I felt in my heart that there was something more for me out there, a higher calling, some other way to make a positive impact, something bigger. I didn't know exactly what that new professional path would look like, but I knew I had burned out on what I was doing. It was my bread-and-butter, my main livelihood, but I felt the time had come to shut down my plant medicine school and make room for whatever would come next.

I believed that if I created a vacuum, the Universe would fill that space with something better, that it would guide me and provide for me as I wandered down the dark tunnel of the great unknown and prayed to be given a new path of service. My spirit was ready for a new adventure, but at the same time, my rational mind felt very anxious about this approach.

While another person might have sought out a part-time job to supplement their income during the transition, my heart would not allow me to do that. When I even contemplated walking into a restaurant and applying to be a server, something I had done in college, I felt terribly guilty. It felt very much wrong, as if I were betraying my higher calling and failing to trust Spirit to provide for me. As much as my rational mind did not like this, I knew that enduring great vulnerability was a test I was called to experience willingly as an initiation and demonstration of my sincerity through right action. I believed that if I did stay the course despite the discomfort involved, the process would purify my ego and forge my heart with fortitude.

Sometimes the capacity of the psyche doesn't match the courage of the heart. I wasn't sleeping so well. My mind spiraled in anxiety about my finances late at night. Could the income stream from my healing work really be enough? Could I even handle doing more of it, given that it took a lot out of me emotionally to do that very deep work? I am an introvert, not an extrovert. How would this all work out?

Kambo sounded interesting. Maybe it could help me. I did like that it is a shamanic medicine from the Amazon rainforest. That was my style.

"What does this kambo cleanse involve?" I asked Kate.

As it turned out, quite a lot. Kate said I would need to fast overnight for twelve hours, and then for the treatment itself, I would first need to chug nearly a gallon of water, then she would burn my skin with a stick of incense, and finally she'd apply the moistened frog medicine to my raw burns, at which time my heart would race and I would feel awfully sick and vomit violently for about an hour. And she said I should go through this process three days in a row for optimal results.

"Um, no thanks," I told her. "I don't like to throw up. I haven't even thrown up on ayahuasca."

But then I went out hiking near the Willamette River, and as I walked along a path that encircled a small pond, a crowd of tiny little frogs swarmed around me. A few days later I went hiking at the Columbia River and came upon a huge cacophony of big croaking frogs. They sang loudly and for a long time, and with such urgency, that it was almost eerie. Clearly, I was being called.

So I told Kate, "OK, I'll do it."

She knocked on my door in the morning, and when I opened it, I saw she was holding a plastic bucket. I knew what that was for, and I felt intimidated. Was I really going to do this?

"Come on in," I said.

Kate was in her late thirties, tall and thin with bright green eyes and curly salt-and-pepper hair. Her posture was very straight, her demeanor polite yet reserved, her movements fluid and meticulous. She dressed in fitted lace and flowing, stretchy fabrics in dark jewel tones that evoked a gypsy priestess vibe.

We sat on the carpet together in my meditation space, which was in my bedroom. She burned Palo Santo and invited me to set a strong intention for the kambo purge process.

"I want to clear away my ego's resistance to following divine will," I said. "I want to trust my path more."

She had me drink the water very quickly, within ten minutes. This was uncomfortable, nauseating and difficult. Then she lit a stick of incense and burned five dots into the skin between my ankle and lower calf, which was painful. Then she sprayed water on a stick of medicine and scraped at it with a small knife until she had some gooey yellow blobs on the end of the blade. She applied them to my burns, which she called "gates."

As the medicine came on, she sang shamanic melodies in languages unfamiliar to me and beat a hide drum. My heart pounded. My face and ears got very hot, my hands swelled red with blood, and my throat felt tight. It was difficult to breathe.

"Raise your chin," she said. I did; it helped some.

I felt very sick but I was afraid to throw up, so I suppressed the urge, which only seemed to prolong my suffering. The worst of the ordeal was over within an hour but the rest of the day my face looked very puffy and I felt terrible, like I had the flu.

Kate came back the next morning, and we got ready to repeat the same process, except she added even more medicine this time. "Talk me into it," I told her.

"You don't have to do it today," she said.

"Yes, I do," I sighed. "I know I'm being called."

This second time she applied the kambo, I allowed myself to actually throw up, and fortunately I felt much better afterwards.

The following morning we did the third treatment, and that was smoother too. Kate coached me to use mindfulness and focus on the sensations in my body during the process, as well as to sense the stuck energy within myself and cast it out with the water when the waves of sickness came. As I heeded her guidance, I felt the cleansing catharsis of the purge.

She looked into the bucket and told me that the various colors inside of it reflected the organs from which the substances had emerged, and that they also corresponded to various emotions. In Traditional Chinese Medicine, the organs are understood to store emotional excesses. When someone has a lot of pent up anger, for instance, it gets stored in the liver. When there is grief, it is held in the lungs, and it comes out as white phlegm. That's what I released.

When it was over, Kate said the benefits would reveal themselves in the coming days.

Indeed, they did. The anxiety disappeared, I slept soundly again, I felt cheerful and centered and courageous, and I had a strong desire to meditate for hours. It was quite a lovely state to be in.

After about two and a half weeks, however, the doubts and fears about this bold move I had made in my professional life came back. And so did the frog omens.

I opened the local alt-weekly newspaper and saw an ad with a full-page photo of a frog. I stopped at a traffic light and saw a huge mural of a frog on the side of a building. Once again, the call was there.

We did another set of treatments. These were painful, too, and I had to overcome my natural aversion to discomfort to get myself to go through with them, but I took heart in something Pema Chodron has said: "Courage isn't the absence of fear. It is feeling the fear and doing it anyway."

The frog omens kept coming. A friend who didn't know about my kambo journey handed me two little crystals shaped like frogs after her intuitive healing session with me, saying, "I thought you would like these." I was amazed. She had just unknowingly told me to get two more kambo treatments.

After each ceremony I felt lighter, like kambo was casting out the sadness that had long ago crystalized into a mild yet chronic depression, weighing down my psyche like a cloud of ice.

I sensed that this grief I was purging came not only from my own suffering – from childhood trauma, from romantic heartbreaks, and so on – but also from other lifetimes and other people, including my ancestors. It even felt to me, intuitively, as though enduring this process was purifying my karma. Sometimes, it felt even bigger and deeper than that.

I liked to wear my "I Stand With Standing Rock" T-shirt when I sat through my kambo treatments, in solidarity for the cause. My heart swelled with deep respect for the warrior activists who were enduring the pain of frigid temperatures in the winter in South Dakota – and, sadly, sometimes being cruelly abused by police forces – to stand up for Mother Earth and protect the wilderness from an oil pipeline that was at risk of causing harm to their land and water. All of this was happening at the same time as my initiations. I hoped that perhaps my kambo work could reverberate out into the cosmic field and make some kind of impact for the better, and somehow support them spiritually.

The kambo treatments amplified my sensitivities such that I became even more aware of the subtle realms of energy, so much so that from within my own apartment, I could now physically feel the electromagnetic field generated by my downstairs neighbor's TV, which produced an uncomfortable buzzing sensation in my body when it was turned on.

Kambo also brought me some extremely vivid, mystical dreams that somehow felt even more real to me than waking life.

In one, I sat in a restaurant booth with friends, looking out the window upon a plain, because I saw a herd of bison in the distance. Suddenly, a buffalo turned and charged several hundred yards towards the building, breaking the glass and landing directly on the table! I froze, feeling both awe and fear at being in the presence of this very large, wild animal. And then the buffalo turned to face me.

My heart pounded and I felt just as overwhelmed and shocked as I would if this had happened in waking life. It felt extremely real.

The buffalo pressed his forehead against my own. As he did this he radiated great love and respect from his heart to mine.

My mind went into a chatter of excitement, as minds will do when we feel overwhelmed and shocked, but then I heard Maestro's voice cut through it, saying, "Receive," and it went silent. I felt an electrical current flow from the buffalo's head directly into my third eye and then down my spine.

When I awoke, I wondered what this blessing symbolized. I looked up the meaning of buffalo in the book *Animal Speak* by Ted Andrews, which catalogs the shamanic symbolism of various animals, and under buffalo was listed: abundance.

In another dream, I walked along a very mountainous, tall, rocky cliff overlooking land below. I suspected that I was somewhere in the Dakotas, although in this life I have never actually been to that region and do not have any firsthand knowledge of how it looks or feels. I saw a number of sticks planted in the ground with colorful pieces of fabric tied to them, and I saw that they were waving in the wind. Though I had never seen or heard of anything like them before, I somehow knew intuitively that they were called prayer ties, and that they had been placed symbolically in a sacred place at a high elevation so that the prayers they contained could be seen and heard by Heaven.

When I looked down at my hands in the dream, I saw that I was carrying a gigantic white feather as I walked along this cliff. It was so large that it could belong to no living bird. I got the feeling that this feather symbolized Heaven's reply.

This dream has stuck with me for years. I wondered to which culture those prayer ties belonged. For some reason, I didn't actually research it until six years later when I was writing this book. And the answer, I discovered, is that it is a Lakota tradition. When I looked up where the Lakota tribe lives, I learned that they are a subset of the Sioux and have reservations in North and South Dakota, including Standing Rock.

15

THE COSMIC MIRROR

Nine months into my journey with kambo, I was no longer able to afford the rent for the one-bedroom apartment I had lived in for nine years, so I did what I had to do: gave away most of my possessions and prepared to downsize, to move in with roommates. It's said that when one door closes, another one opens, and that was certainly true for me: As it happened, at the very same time as I got an eviction warning, a small second-floor bedroom became available for rent at Kate's house.

This was really good news, because Kate was the only person I knew who would rent a room to someone like me who had a totally unpredictable income stream. But she understood. She knew I was doing what I was called to do, and that it came at a cost.

Kate's place was a Victorian house whose exterior was painted a vibrant royal purple, located in southeast Portland near Laurelhurst Park, which was a really cute, hip neighborhood. My new bedroom just happened to be decorated in an aesthetic suited to my taste. The walls were painted my favorite shade of lavender, and on one of them someone had painted a whimsical tree in shimmering metallic tones. It had a nice hardwood floor, and shiny silver stars dangled like mirrors on thin fishing wire from the ceiling. Even the door had a little touch that felt like it was made for me: a golden flourish over the arch.

This move was very obviously aligned, yet it was still a challenging adjustment. I had lived alone in my one-bedroom apartment for a long time, about nine years, and now I would have just a small room and five roommates.

It was an eclectic assortment of personalities, to put things politely. Two people were hardcore binge-drinkers with no interest whatsoever in spirituality, while the rest of us were highly sensitive, health-conscious energy healers. In the morning hours, we could all hear the sounds of weeping, purging and retching coming from the basement, along with the reverberations of an animal-skin drum shaking the walls, because that's when Kate was facilitating kambo ceremonies. As we wandered downstairs to the kitchen in our pajamas, we passed by her clients, who we saw constantly streaming in and out of the house. It felt as if we were living in the middle of a kambo clinic – because essentially, we were.

It was not a quiet environment, nor a peaceful one. There were conflicts between all of us. In other words, learning experiences.

I was very grateful to have spent some time in Twelve Step rooms, where I learned the saying, "When one finger points forward, three others point back at you." Similarly, I knew the veracity of the metaphysical rule known as the Law of Attraction, which says that everything we experience in our reality is in some way a reflection of something within us, whether conscious or subconscious. So I knew that these conflicts were rich with value for personal growth and spiritual evolution, and I had plenty to ponder.

When things got difficult, I would ask myself, "What does this remind me of from the past?" and then I could see that the dynamics of my current circumstances were very much like old patterns of dysfunction that I had experienced in childhood, and in re-experiencing echoes of them, I could recognize particular aspects of unresolved emotional baggage I was still carrying from the past. These gems of awareness formed the intentions with which I would then purify myself with the frog medicine, thus purging the past. As soon as I did a ceremony, I got to watch the external circumstances effortlessly shift to become a reflection of my newly cleansed and upgraded energetic blueprints.

For example, we had one roommate in the house who was frequently intoxicated, radiating a lot of negative energy, anger and depression. He was unkind to my dog, so she growled at him, and I didn't blame her. Being around this person was frustrating and unpleasant, and both of us refused to move out. I had nowhere to go, and I guess he felt similarly. I knew this stuckness was happening on purpose, because everything happens on purpose. So I asked myself, "When have I felt stuck in a toxic situation like this before?" I was able to connect the many layers of emotions triggered by this situation to previous experiences in childhood that had felt similar. I purged it all out in a kambo ceremony, after which the roommate suddenly had a change of heart and moved out of the house. I was not surprised at this outcome. I had assumed that very result would occur once I had cleared the stuff from my energy field that resonated with him, because he would no longer be a reflection and would therefore have to disappear from my reality. It was spiritual alchemy.

The new roommate who moved in was a mirror, too. This guy was much easier to be around, friendlier, kinder, and with a good sense of humor. He was quirky though, and in particular something that really bugged me was how he constantly listened to talk radio and podcasts all day long, and all night, too, wherever he went. I could hear it buzzing from his bedroom, which was next door to mine, and even when he walked around the house or cooked something, he brought a speaker with him. He really never turned off the incessant sound. I thought it was so odd that this person never gave himself a moment of silence.

It annoyed me, so I asked myself, "In what way is this person a reflection of my own consciousness? I don't listen to podcasts all day long, but what is it that's similar that I do and don't realize right now?" And the answer that arose within me was that actually, my own mind was always chattering, too. I was always listening to my thoughts. All day long, and all night long, I was thinking. There was no silence inside my own head! What a valuable insight that was. So, I resolved to meditate more. Later that day I saw that roommate in the kitchen, where he was cooking dinner. Out of nowhere, he announced to me that he'd just had an epiphany: He wanted to improve his life by turning off his radio sometimes and giving himself some time to experience pure silence![3]

I have seen over and over again how transforming my inner world creates external change. This has been true not just in my own life, but also in the lives of the many people who have come to me for intuitive healing and counseling over the years. I could fill a book just with stories about that. Here are just a few:

A woman came to me because she wanted metaphysical assistance with receiving money; her pension payments kept getting snagged by red tape. We found that she had a psychological block in which deep down she did not feel deserving of having her needs met. We cleared it in a couple of hours with some deep spiritual counseling and Reiki energy healing. She immediately got her money right after the session, because the mirror of her life shifted to reflect her inner decluttering.

Another person came to see me for Reiki healing because she wanted help with a terrible recurring pattern: She was stuck in a job

---

[3]   I had another roommate, at a different time, who used to send me really unkind, critical text messages momentarily whenever I had critical thoughts towards myself. She really helped me gain control of my Inner Critic because whenever I gave it a microphone in my own mind, this Outer Abuser gave it an external voice. Of course, once I realized what was happening, I saw that I couldn't give any more air time to negativity in my head. I had wanted to move out, but couldn't find a room. Yet as soon as I finally managed to ignore the inner critic in my head, a desirable room instantly opened up for me at a new, nicer place with friendlier people who resonated with my kinder mental environment.

with a very sadistic boss who took pleasure in messing with her and trying to make her cry. Sadly, this had happened many times before. When I asked about her childhood, she said her mother had been very cruel, pranking her in bizarre and demented ways, like faking her own death and laying on the floor with ketchup as a practical joke, and enjoying making her daughter cry. I used Reiki to heal her inner child and release this energetic pattern of psychopathic abuse that had imprinted itself as normal in her mind and in her energy field. She came back a week later and told me the boss had abruptly quit right after our session and not only that, now she was actually getting a promotion! Naturally, her life experiences were simply reflecting the internal transformation.

I've seen so many seemingly miraculous changes occur that I haven't the faintest doubt in the veracity of the Law of Attraction, or as I like to call it, the cosmic mirror. While many people may doubt it, this is only because they have only a superficial understanding of how it works. It is not the case that simply changing one's conscious thoughts to more positive ones is necessarily sufficient to magnetize better things into your life. Often it takes resolving the emotional wounds of the past, as well, and sometimes this even requires healing historical traumas embedded in one's ancestral lineage. Alchemy is assured when the root cause of an unhappy pattern is addressed.

***

After six months of living there, and eighteen months or so of my kambo journey, I had received thirty-three kambo ceremonies from Kate, and I sensed that this was the end of our work together. But one day, I could feel something within myself asking for purification. So I had an idea. I had once read that shamans of the jungle sometimes heal their clients just by singing the songs that vibrationally match the physical medicines they use. I asked Kate if she wanted to experiment with this and try it, to see if we could do kambo without kambo. Kate said yes.

I fasted for twelve hours before the ceremony as usual and we did everything we usually did except apply the frog resin. I drank a half gallon of water within ten minutes, we set intentions for purification, and Kate lit a stick of Palo Santo, wafting it around the air.

As she sang her kambo medicine songs, I wondered if anything would happen or if I would purge. I didn't feel nauseated and figured it wasn't going to happen, but after ten minutes or so I suddenly puked. Instead of water, I was shocked to see that the liquid inside the plastic bucket was a deep, dark brown color. I felt shifted inside, too. The vibration of kambo was so strong in both of us that we hadn't needed the physical substance to access the alchemy of the frog.

We were both amazed.

16

EAGLE FEATHERS

Horse is the second shaman I drank ayahuasca with. I call him Horse because he coughs a lot, and when he coughs it sounds like neighing.

Like Maestro, Horse is also an American-born shaman who trained with indigenous teachers in the Peruvian Amazon. He facilitated ayahuasca retreats there, but in America he also secretly led ceremonies at his rural homestead. I had heard about him from a mutual friend who had attended one of his lectures on herbal medicine. She said good things about her ceremonial experiences with him, and showed me his picture so I could see if I resonated with his energy. He was a blonde guy about the same age as me – in his mid thirties – with a thin build and a studious, bespectacled appearance. What was most important to me was that in his smiling, shining eyes I could sense his spirit, and I felt it was genuine, filled with good intentions.

When an invitation came to drink ayahuasca with Horse, I signed up because I wanted to receive divine instructions about the next steps on my path of service to a higher purpose. My heart burned with the desire to find some new way to contribute to the healing of this world.

I prepared for the ceremony by doing silent meditations in which I would breathe into my heart space and sit with the intention of listening. But this time, as an offering to the divine, I did something different than just send blessings of Reiki to *Madre* as I had in the past.

I knew that Spirit speaks the language of energy. Prayers with words are powerful, but prayers of pure emotion and symbolic, intentional action can be even moreso. That is why, each morning, I placed my hands in prayer position at my heart and welled up a feeling of deep love, respect and appreciation for Mother Earth, as an offering and a gift, and so that she could know my sincere desire to help her, and then I bowed down in the yoga position known as child's pose, sublimating myself to Her, and to the higher divine feminine, the cosmic mother that she is in an emanation of, as a demonstration of my intention of submission and service to divine will. I did this for months before the day arrived.

The ceremony was held in a rustic wooden house that reminded me of a treehouse, because it was elevated above a lush flower-and-herb garden and surrounded by tall Douglas fir trees.

Inside, brightly colored psychedelic prints made by Amazonian artists hung on the walls. The elevated living room, where everyone had gathered, had floor-to-ceiling windows and a big wooden deck surrounding it.

I felt very grateful to be there. It seemed almost like a miracle that I was, because some force had sent a gauntlet of obstacles to block my way that morning. First the dog sitter canceled at the last minute, so then I drove my dog, Daisy, to a friend's house, but the friend's dog attacked her and drew blood. It was already afternoon by then and I was supposed to be at the ceremony in two hours and it was about an hour's drive away. Amazingly, using a phone app, I was able to find a sitter, but then I hit so much traffic that I almost didn't make it on time before they were going to lock the door. When I finally arrived, everyone was already on their meditation cushions, getting ready to begin.

To open the ceremony, Horse lit a small bundle of *mapacho*, Amazonian tobacco, rolled in leaves like a joint. He inhaled deeply into his lungs, held it there in his heart with closed eyes, concentrating his intention in to it, and then exhaled the smoke with a great sweeping arm motion, as if he were firing prayers to Heaven.

Horse, like Maestro, had two assistants with him to help. One was a tall, handsome ex-soldier with a very serious demeanor, and the other was a petite elder woman who radiated joy and lightness of being as she flitted around the room, greeting everyone with love. She reminded me of a hummingbird. She used her energy to work in the sun as a construction laborer by day, but on nights and weekends, she served her community as a death doula, a spiritual midwife for the departing.

When the ayahuasca came on, I felt an intense wave of fear and inner resistance. It was so overwhelming that I couldn't let go, despite how much I wanted to, and despite how diligently I had practiced meditating beforehand. Everyone was supposed to observe a strict code of "noble silence" unless we needed assistance. I did, so I said, "Help!"

First the ex-soldier came and smudged me with burning sage. I heard a gentle rustling sound as he wafted the smoke with a dried chakapa-leaf fan, and then the hummingbird woman came and crouched down next to me.

"I think I'm dying," I whispered to her.

"You're not dying," she said, nearly laughing. "I have sat in more than a hundred ayahuasca ceremonies. I assure you, you are not *actually* dying."

"I hear you, but I really feel like I am," I said.

"That's okay," she said.

"How is that okay?" I asked.

"Sometimes, it's good to die," she said.

"Sometimes it's good to die," I repeated. Her words resonated and her peace with death became my own. She gently stood up and left me to my solitude.

If I was dying in this moment, there was nothing I could do but embrace it, so I did.

I died, and dying felt like slipping away, surrendering the body, surrendering all sense of the known. But I was surprised that I did not lose my consciousness at all.

Death was only a passageway. It was not the end of being, nor of experiencing, nor even of knowing. I felt my body decay and merge into the rich soil of a forest, and I felt a very pleasurable sensation of oneness as it was subsumed by the diverse web of sentient, vitally alive fungi, microorganisms and plant matter. Death was a gloriously satisfying new depth of connection with Mother Earth. Communing with her radiating energies of unconditional love and peace, and taking them in at the deepest, most atomic level of being, was immensely soothing, and actually, downright delightful.

A phrase echoed through my consciousness: "There is no Self."

Before my eyes I saw all of reality reduced to the ground of pure being: a vibrating electromagnetic field, distinguished into the appearance of form via a variation in the frequency and densities of energy. I felt I was underneath this field somehow, looking up at it.

And then the vision morphed and I saw *Madre Ayahuasca* weaving the strands of my DNA together with those of the planet's indigenous people, ancestors who lived long ago, and a vast tapestry of plant and animal consciousness. It looked as if I were becoming an embodiment of the Earth herself.

Next I was reborn. I burst up through my own pelvis and stood atop the dead body that had contained my old identity, like Kali, or like a cordyceps mushroom exploding out of a caterpillar.

I rested then and listened as Horse sang *icaros*, melodies in Spanish celebrating the waters, the plants, and the stars. He sang of the eagle and the condor flying. He sang catchy, rhythmic praises to ayahuasca. He sang appeals to Great Spirit to heal our hearts. He sang songs reminding us to heed the wisdom of the ancestors.

The lyrics were very beautiful, but I noticed that his voice sounded a little bit off-key at times. As soon as I had this thought, *Madre Ayahuasca* guided me to reverse that judgment and instead intentionally project the belief that he was a skilled vocalist. As I did this, I was amazed to observe that his singing improved markedly! And I could feel Her pleasure as I began to understand that the way I perceived the world around me, including other people, exerts a creative force. [4]

Under her influence, I was able to observe the other participants with much-heightened psychic perception such that I could perceive the specifics of what they were going through, the lessons and issues they were clearing and processing. It was clear as glass to see right into them through the telepathic field created by our shared experience of altered consciousness. With wonder I saw Horse and his male assistant vomit out the energy of pollution, purging for the planet with their bodies as proxies.[5] I understood then that ayahuasca ceremonies are not just opportunities for us as individuals to seek visionary experiences, spiritual growth or the expansion of consciousness. They are also alchemical rituals for planetary healing.

---

[4]   Later, I learned that there really have been scientific studies verifying the impact of the observer on musical performances. In experiments, when the audience was instructed to think positive thoughts about them, orchestral musicians performed objectively better than when the audience thought negative thoughts. I see this as an extension of what we are learning is the key feature of quantum reality: Our consciousness has a very real creative impact, not only on minute particles and waves but on people, too.

[5]   I found out later when I heard people share their experiences that my perceptions had been accurate.

It could seem that the velocity of ecological collapse is too massive for us to reverse, except that it's possible to shift it through the quantum field, the realm of miracles. I received a cosmic download, an inner knowing, that some of us, including myself, had been metaphysically weighted by the divine for the benefit of humanity, such that we became like armies unto ourselves, forces with such power that our individual actions were like those of thousands of people, and so that when we did something loving for another, it would affect the greater karma and shared manifestation of our species for the better. In this way, we really could change the world, even if we were few in number.

As Horse sang his last *icaros* and brought the ceremony to a close, he said, "This ceremony is coming to an end, but the ceremony of the rest of your life is just beginning."

I received one last psychic message. A council of ancestors spoke through one authoritative male voice, transmitting two distinct messages in a commanding tone, as if dispensing marching orders. The council said: "Speak," and "Eagle Feathers."

When the ceremony was over, I told Hummingbird about this, and she smiled and showed me her own eagle feathers, which she had pinned up to hang above her seat.

"What does it mean?" I asked her.

"Tara, my emerald gem," she said, "That is for you to find out."

Later, I read that in Native American cultures, eagle feathers are awarded by a tribal council to a warrior in recognition of bravery. They are considered the highest honor.

17

TOAD MEDICINE

About six months later, an author friend invited me to give a lecture at a psychedelics conference in Southern Oregon. As I drove down the highway to present a talk about how kambo, cannabis, and ayahuasca can help heal the world, I was struck with the strong intuition that someone there was going to offer me a chance to experience the medicine of the Sonoran Desert Toad. This toad is the *Bufo alvarius* species, the skin of which exudes a natural source of 5-MEO DMT, a highly potent entheogen. I knew very little about the toad, but I knew there were going to be several lectures about it and I was quite curious.

When I stepped on the stage to present my lecture, I felt joy and deep satisfaction in my heart. The words flowed with ease. I spoke for twenty minutes. The title of my talk was "Cleansing the Ego with Cannabis, Kambo and Ayahuasca."

In this lecture, I shared my philosophy on what the sacred medicines are all about and why they are in our lives, from a metaphysical perspective. I also shared the story of a powerful experience I had during an ayahuasca retreat that taught me what it means to really be in service – ceremonies which I haven't yet recounted in this book.

I began:

"Humanity has an ego imbalance. At its most extreme, the ego convinces us that we are separate from everybody else and everything else, and that nature is an object to be used like a tool.

Ego is resistance to something greater. Ego is resistance to the benevolent, creative force that pervades all things. Ego is separation consciousness.

Ego, as we know, is useful for our concept of self and for being a human walking around. It's not bad in and of itself. It's bad if it's imbalanced. It's problematic, I should say, if it is imbalanced. And when we have an imbalanced ego, some symptoms that we experience are attachment, the need to control, and the inability to trust life. We experience ourselves judging and blaming. We feel like victims. We experience hopelessness. This is an imbalanced ego.

As within, so without. Humanity has an ego imbalance and that's why we have an ecological crisis on the planet at this time…And because the ego imbalance of humanity is so impactful on the rest of the planet, you know we really are not alone in our desire to heal. We really are not alone in our desire to heal the planet. The Earth is sending her medicines to us. The Earth's medicines are calling to us, and these are the entheogens. These are the plant medicines. These are the animal medicines. They are coming and they are calling for us because they have the power to transform our consciousness. They have the power to balance the ego. They have the power to help us connect with that creative, benevolent force that guides all things, that pervades all things.

And in this talk, I want to share with you how we can work with three very, very powerful medicines in particular who are, in my personal experience, experts at helping humanity clear the ego – clear the imbalances of the ego – and these three medicines we're going to be speaking about today are kambo, ayahuasca, and cannabis…

Let me begin by talking about ayahuasca because ayahuasca is, I think, the most well-known of ego destroyers. Ayahuasca really is a guru teacher more than anything. She is omnipotent. She is omniscient. She desires for us to become our best selves. She loves humanity, actually. And as a plant spirit, she wants to see us grow and evolve into our greatest capacity. And she believes that we're capable of so much more and that is why when you go to sit with ayahuasca, she confronts you with all of your shadows, and with all of the things that you don't want to see, and all of the hardest things that you have to face. And it's why as well she asks us to die, egoically speaking.

I had a really powerful experience – and that's putting it mildly – with ayahuasca, and…I'm coming from the perspective of having sat with two really fantastic Shipibo trained shamans, really amazing people who are dedicated and who are essentially yogis. Their whole lives are dedicated to the plants. I do believe that the experience we have with these medicines is very much dependent upon the consciousness level of the people we have the experience with. So I'm coming from this perspective and I'm very lucky.

So, I experienced in this one especially impactful ayahuasca ceremony that in my first night with Her, She showed me my ego. I had a hard time surrendering and allowing this medicine to come in. And I spent the whole night in an internal battle of resistance, wanting to surrender and unable to surrender: Thinking, frustrated with the facilitators, because they were taken under with medicine and they couldn't sing because they were having such a hard ride. And I was feeling frustrated. And I wanted to do something, but there wasn't anything I *could* do. And I was experiencing, empathically, the feeling of anxiety as I could hear and see that people all around me were struggling and suffering, and experiencing pain and crying and throwing up, and I wanted, in some way, to change the experience. And so finally, I realized what I needed to do was ask, 'How can I serve?' And so I asked the plant, 'How can I serve? What can I do?'

Finally, I cared more about the people around me than my own experience of being frustrated and annoyed that there weren't songs, annoyed that I wasn't having visions. And the plant shot light through me like a fire hose. And I lit up. And then the songs began and the whole ceremony lifted! It was really amazing.

And then the next night I had this experience of completely choosing to be of service, choosing to care about how it was impacting everyone around me, choosing actively to be a conduit for good, and in that experience I breathed into my heart and I began to realize that the facilitators of the ceremony were speaking to me telepathically. They were saying, 'Go back and breathe in your heart. You're thinking too much, you're too loud, you can't hear anybody.' And so I went and I listened to what they said and I returned to the breath. And I realized they really could hear me. So I said in my head, 'Please come over to me,' and they did. They came over to me *physically* and they took my hands, and all of a sudden I entered into a bliss state and I experienced interconnectedness with the web of light. And I realized, 'Whoa, this is what happens if I'm not in my ego! Wow, what potential!'

I came away with three messages from the plant. The messages were: 'Love everybody. Forgive everybody. And don't complain. Love everybody, forgive everybody, and don't complain.' And I understood that these were instructions for how to cleanse the ego. I have work to do. It's not enough to have a powerful experience in ceremony. Of course, we then have work to do, we have to follow the instructions of our guru teachers, these plants, these amazing medicines.

And so I immediately got to work with that. And I realized if I want to love everybody, really what I need to do is love all parts of myself, because everyone I experience, I experience as a reflection of myself. If I want to forgive everybody, not only do I need to forgive myself for anything, but I also need to release all of the pain, emotional pain that I've been holding on to from any past experiences that were hurting me still because as long as we are suffering, we're angry about it. And I realized that forgiveness is really a side effect of releasing all of our pain – processing, experiencing, and witnessing our pain.

And then, 'Don't complain,' that's actually the hardest. That's actually the hardest because that's what the ego wants to do. The ego wants to say, 'Things should be different than they are; I want to fix it.' 'Don't complain' means radical acceptance. Reminds me of a friend of mine. He goes to an ashram in India, and he tells me that in the ashram no matter what happens to you – you could show up and have something very tragic just happen – they'll congratulate you. 'Oh, congratulations. That's wonderful.' Because everything is material for awakening. Everything is useful. Everything is as it needs to be.

So I came away from the ceremony and I worked with intuitive healers very intensively. I am one myself and I've already been on this path, but I worked even more intensively because I thought, 'Wow, I could be telepathic! I can experience bliss! And, more important than anything, I can make a positive impact on everyone around me if I can get out of my ego!'"

I touched on kambo and cannabis in this talk as well. Of cannabis, I said, "Cannabis is a plant that elevates our vibrational state and helps us to understand ourselves. It's an amplifier of the shadow. In order to love everybody, we have to love ourselves. In order to love ourselves, we have to know ourselves. In order to heal ourselves, we have to know what needs healing. This is where cannabis can come in, in such a valuable and important way."

I ended the talk by saying, "Humanity has an ego imbalance. And as we heal ourselves, we heal the planet. As we clear our pain, we clear the ego. The ego is made up of pain. And we're not alone in this task. Medicines are coming to us and medicines are calling to us. Medicines themselves want to evolve human consciousness… These medicines are intelligent. They are emanations of the Earth herself. The Earth knows what she's doing. And she seeks to heal herself, by healing us."

As soon as I stepped off the stage, a well-dressed, elegant blonde woman with long, dangling feather earrings walked over to approach me. She had grace, kindness and respect shining out of her eyes, and when she spoke to introduce herself, it was with a delightful German accent.

"I am a medicine woman also," she said. "I carry Bufo and if you are open to it, I would like to give you a private ceremony tomorrow."

"I would love that," I told her. "Thank you."

I was very curious to see what the toad medicine would be like.

At the conference, multiple speakers spoke with great reverence about *Bufo alvarius*, and how intriguing it is that this unique, sacred medicine seems to have suddenly emerged at Earth's time of need. While some people suspect that toad medicine was used long ago by the indigenous people of Central America, because it appears in cave paintings, it is not part of any living tradition, at least as far as any researchers have determined. As a result, those who facilitate toad ceremonies today are very much trailblazers and innovators. Some use it to bring breakthroughs in emotional healing for their clients, but it's more commonly viewed as a tool to rocket-launch yourself into an illuminated state of spiritual awakening.

The toad has a reputation for producing a very brief but profound experience of oneness with the divine, a sense of merging to such an extent that recipients frequently have the epiphany that they really are God – that God is incarnated within them. Many spiritual traditions teach that God is inside of everyone, but this is a felt experience.

Is it good that anyone can now attain what used to be a rare pinnacle of mystical enlightenment? Within the psychedelic community, some believe it is the critical missing piece that will deliver humanity from our materialistic stupor. But others talk about how, on the other hand, it can have the paradoxical effect of massively inflating the ego of unprepared minds and leave a person with a God complex. As psychedelic author Martin W. Ball has said about this, the realization one has to come to is, "Yes, you are God. But so is everybody else."

The next day, I had a chance to experience this myself.

My new friend, the German medicine woman, sat across from me on the floor of a bedroom she had sanctified with sage smoke and flowers. She held a glass object that looked like a lightbulb to me. When I asked if that is what it was, she said in her gorgeous accent, "No, actually it's a crack pipe. We will use it to smoke the toad medicine."

I laughed. "Ok then!"

"When I smoke the medicine, I become one with the toad," she said. "I will even look like one."

It was true. After she inhaled, her pupils dilated and she squatted in a funny, toad-like position as the spirit came into her body. She moved very close to me and instructed me to look into her eyes, and not to break the gaze, which she held for an indeterminate period of time that felt uncomfortably long.

While she looked into my soul she moved her hands in the air in front of my heart as if unwinding a tangled knot.

"Ouch," she said. "There are a *lot* of scars here."

For sure, that was true. My heart felt weary and calloused from the many years of emotional trauma I had been through in this life, and it had hardened me. However many layers I had been able to clear by purging with kambo and receiving thousands of hours of shamanic and Reiki healings, apparently there was still more residue, and now she was clearing it away.

When the medicine wore off for her, she filled the pipe with more of the secretion of the Bufo toad and she guided me to inhale as she lit it with a torch.

My lungs hurt from the dry hot smoke and the toad medicine came on very suddenly. I saw golden light everywhere and had an overwhelming awareness of being God, or more accurately, a feeling that God was being me. It was very much a mind-blowing revelation, and lasted perhaps ten minutes.

This was, as far as I have been told, the quintessential toad experience. For me, it was an awakening into the magnitude of the power and responsibility I carry in this world as a human being, and of the potential we each have to become divine vessels, to serve the highest good as conduits for miracles.

18

MEETING MY TEACHER

W hen I spoke about my experiences with kambo, people sometimes asked if I would give them treatments myself, as a practitioner. I felt touched that they would trust me to facilitate something so sacred and intimate and vulnerable as a kambo ceremony, but I declined, because in my heart I felt that it would not be appropriate. Serving a sacred medicine is a position bestowed by divine appointment. It is not something one chooses oneself, even if you are a talented intuitive healer and ceremonialist in whom others sense capability. There are reasons for this. When a person gives kambo to another, there is a spiritual and energetic exchange, an activation that takes place, and so the practitioner's energy must be ready. It must be initiated; pure, clean, and divinely designated for such work. And so I waited. My first step would be to find a teacher. But I knew there would be no need to go looking. When the time was right, my teacher would appear.

I met Kari at an ayahuasca retreat in the Cascade mountains of Washington state. She was there as a kambo practitioner offering the frog medicine to help everyone cleanse their bodies before the ceremony, so that we could be extra sensitive and thus more receptive to the nuances of the subtle realms of spirit. She offered kambo treatments in the mornings after ayahuasca, as well. Of course, I was eager to receive them. I was excited to get kambo from someone other than Kate for the first time, someone who had gone to Brazil to learn about the medicine firsthand from indigenous healers in the Huni Kuin tribe, also called the Kaxinawa.

Kari has a striking appearance. She was in her twenties, pretty and olive-skinned, with big brown eyes and cascades of straight, shiny platinum hair down to her waist. She has a humble yet confident way of carrying herself, unassuming yet strong, and her energy is a little bit androgynous. She is on the quiet side. I really liked the way she began her kambo ceremonies with deep and earnest prayers, speaking with great reverence and sincerity as she says, "Thank you, Great Spirit. Thank you," to the celestial bodies, to Mother Earth, to Father Sky, and you could feel her heart in all of it. After she applied the medicine to my skin, she sat in silence or sang some short medicine songs and shook a rawhide rattle to help break up stuck energy as I purged.

Kari was happy to give kambo treatments to me, and because I already had plenty of experience with it, she asked if I would be her assistant and help her with her larger group ceremonies that weekend at the ayahuasca retreat. My job would be to help people make it to and from the bathroom when they were in the midst of their purging, to cleanse the energy in the room with dried sage and Palo Santo when she was singing her songs, and to help reassure them that they were going to be OK, that the sickness would pass. Having been in their shoes many times before, I felt confident I could do that. It was easy. I felt great respect for Kari and I was delighted to be her helper. I couldn't imagine anyone more perfect for me to learn from.

Much later, under the influence of the plant medicine, I looked at Kari and was struck by a sudden inner knowing – a claircognizant hit – that she had been a famous saint in one of her past lives. When I asked if anyone had ever told her before that she was the reincarnation of this particular individual, she said that yes, she had heard this before. The saint she used to be was Mother Teresa.

Kari and I stayed in touch.

A couple of months after we met, there came a day when I felt I needed kambo, but there wasn't a practitioner around whom I wanted to get a treatment from. Kate and I had parted ways, and the other local practitioners I knew didn't feel like the right people for me. Kari and I lived far from each other, in different states. So I didn't know what to do. I called her up and we talked about it.

"Honestly, dude, at this point you've had more treatments than most practitioners," Kari said. (She talks like a surfer). "Why don't I send you some kambo and you give it to yourself?"

"Really?" I said. This idea of self-treating had never occurred to me. "You think I can handle it?"

"Definitely, dude," she said. "I can teach you whatever you need to know."

And that's how Kari became my kambo mentor.

She told me to go get a specific type of incense stick to use for burning the skin and removing the top layer, which is how the medicine gets into the body. Quite synchronistically, the brand she recommended was Tara Healing Incense.

When her package arrived, I opened it and found a thin, flat piece of wood coated with white resin. This was kambo that had been gathered by the Matses tribe.

The Matses people are well-known in the kambo world; they are an indigenous group in Peru that were isolated in the jungle until very recently. They were one of the last tribes to be contacted by Western civilization in the late Twentieth Century, and the first known to provide kambo to a white person, who was the journalist Peter Gorman, author of *Sapo In My Soul*, among other books. (Kambo is sometimes called "Sapo," even though Sapo actually means toad in Spanish, because of translation hiccups between cultures).

I placed the kambo stick on my altar and set about creating a sacred space. I burned sage, blessed the floor, ceiling, and walls with Reiki symbols, thanked the frog, and asked it to cleanse my body, my heart and my spirit.

I lit a stick of incense and burned my lower leg, making the "gates" for the medicine to enter my body. Next, I drank a half gallon of water as quickly as I could, swallowing it in big gulps over a period of 10 minutes, which I had done so many times before.

I used a spray bottle to apply water on the stick and moisten the resin, and then I used a steel knife to scrape the resulting goo off the bamboo it came on, forming it into tiny balls that would fit into the burn marks I had made.

I called Kari and put her on speaker phone. "Ok dude, I'm about to put the medicine on my skin. Go for it," I said. She shook her rattle and sang medicine songs for me in a tribal language I didn't know.

"Thank you, kambo," I whispered to the frog spirit as I carefully placed the resin on the burns, where I knew it would flow into my lymphatic system, propelled by my swiftly beating heart.

The medicine stung sharply, brightly, and intensely at first, but after a few minutes it faded. Then I got the vasodilating effect, a flash of heat radiating through the body, and my heart thumped faster, culminating with a buzzing in my ears. My face and hands turned red and swelled with blood.

There was a feeling like being on a roller coaster that's climbing up the scaffolding. "It's temporary. It's going to pass," I reminded myself. I tried to take an attitude of curiosity towards the physical sensations arising, because if you resist or avoid them, you miss out on the full benefits of the healing process.

My breath felt a bit squeezed and labored for a few uncomfortable moments, and then my blood pressure dropped and I felt calm. Then there was the nausea of having a stomach filled with water. I spit some phlegm out and felt better, then I purged forcefully, out both ends.

I could feel pressure moving around inside my body as the frog medicine scanned my organ systems and searched for what needed to be balanced, healed or cast out.

When the process felt complete I said goodbye to Kari and lay down on my bed, a futon mattress, to rest.

When I looked in the mirror later, I saw the puffiness in my face had gone, replaced by the lovely radiant glow that always follows a kambo cleanse.

I saw something else in that mirror, too, something new and different in the eyes. I saw empowerment. I saw an initiated woman.

19

SERVING KAMBO

My very first kambo client was a woman I had met at cannabis parties. She was preparing to move across the country and she asked me to give her a kambo cleanse ceremony as a rite of passage, so that she could release the old and make way for the new. She knew of my own journey with the frog medicine and she had already received Reiki healings with me, so she was excited to be my first recipient. I was glad that it would be her, too, because she was someone with whom I felt a close, kindred connection, a person who has a real, deep appreciation for Earth medicines. She was in fact a passionate activist for cannabis, organizing meetings and putting herself in the spotlight as a single mother to try to remove the stigma around the good herb and help others feel comfortable using it as a medicine. She was also very involved in helping victims of domestic violence.

I came to the hotel room where she was staying. We placed a towel on the floor, next to a plastic bucket and a roll of toilet tissue. I blessed the room with Reiki, thanked the frog spirit and asked for her highest good to unfold. I felt ready. I knew the most important thing I needed to offer was a heart-centered presence of compassion and unconditional love, with complete trust in the medicine, and the frog would do the rest.

She was very brave. She saw the impending discomfort as nothing but the labor pain of rebirthing herself. Her treatment was very intense and her face swelled quite a lot, a common side effect known as "frog face."

When she had finished purging I looked at her and suddenly had a vision of her dressed in all-white clothing, and at the same time, I heard the phrase, "White Buffalo Calf Woman." I felt this was her. When I shared this with her, she told me it resonated, and that although she has pale skin, there is Native American blood in her veins. Later I researched who White Buffalo Calf Woman was, and I learned that this was quite synchronistic: White Buffalo Calf Woman was a holy person, a medicine woman, and a prophet who originally taught the Lakota people about the peace pipe. She also taught the men to treat women with respect, and not as sexual objects.[6]

There was one thing about becoming a kambo healer that did give me pause: singing the medicine songs that help activate the physical medicine vibrationally. I was nervous to sing, because I had always been rather tone-deaf. Even when I was just attempting to sing "Happy Birthday" at parties, my voice sometimes would break and I'd feel embarrassed. How was I going to do justice to kambo with a voice like that?

Fortunately, I only had to pray for a miracle to receive one. I asked to be graced with vocal talent so that I could sing medicine songs well as a kambo practitioner. When I next attended an ayahuasca ceremony after that prayer, I opened my mouth and a beautiful melody came out! My voice box was a wind instrument that the plant spirit, *Madre*, was singing through. And as She sang through me, I could feel that She was somehow making tweaks and adjustments, tuning my vocal cords so that they would sound

---

[6]   After she moved, this person became a kambo practitioner and a teacher who trains aspiring healers how to work with other sacred medicines, including ayahuasca vine.

better. I emerged from that ceremony with a strong, on-key singing voice that I actually like the sound of and enjoy sharing. If that is not a miracle, then what is? Heaven furnishes each of its servants with whatever gift is needed to accomplish the mission. I am proof.

My teacher Kari recorded herself singing kambo medicine songs in Spanish and in a tribal language, wrote down the lyrics, and sent them to me. I memorized them and practiced them until I felt confident and ready to share them. I added some English-language medicine songs to sing, as well, such as "Suddhosi Buddhosi" by the artist Shimshai, which goes:

You are forever pure

You are forever true

And the dream of this world

Can never touch you

So give up your attachments

Give up your confusion

And fly to the place

That's beyond all illusion

I arrived at my clients' doorsteps to facilitate kambo ceremonies carrying a vintage horse-leather medicine bag in my hands, with my horse-hide drum slung across my back and my dog Daisy along to share her calm, mellow presence, too. Daisy, a thirty-five pound chihuahua-pitbull mix with a soft fawn-colored coat like a deer, had sat next to me for many of my own kambo treatments. She likes to meditate, and I had initiated her into Reiki as well, so she channels it sometimes. She seems to understand the meaning of ceremony and sits in a dignified, reverent state of relaxed attention when they are happening. In other words, she holds space.

At one of the first homes I visited, I was surprised to see a life-sized statue of Green Tara overlooking the living room, where we held the ceremony. At another, the client offered me an alchemical potion labeled "Green Tara Elixir." The synchronicities abounded.

I amassed a small assortment of kambo sticks from different origins: the Matses tribe at first, and then from a woman who runs a frog preserve in South America and harvests the medicine herself, and from a kambo practitioner colleague of mine who lives in Germany – that one had to travel very far. Each stick has a slightly different feeling to it because it contains a little bit of the energy of each person who gathered it, and also because it comes from different wild frogs who lived in different places. Some sticks came from females and others from males. Even though they're all the same species, each individual has a unique essence and the medicine does, too. I really enjoyed – and still enjoy – matching the frequency of each stick to each individual who comes to me for a treatment.

I learned that it makes a big difference when I talk to the frog spirit before the ceremony and ask it to be gentle. When I do that, usually people have surprisingly soft experiences that are much easier than they expected. When it comes to dosing, I have learned to ask the frog spirit to guide me and to listen intuitively for the right number of dots to burn on someone. The answer comes psychically when I sit in front of my client. The number appears as an image in my mind's eye, or I hear it audibly like a thought that isn't a thought, or I just know. When I sense this number, I share it with my client and ask them to tune into their own intuition and offer consent, so that we can come to a mutual agreement and the dynamic can be an empowering one. I see my role as facilitator, amplifier of intention, witness and guide, and I know that the frog is the healer. I am not there to impose anything; I am there to assist.

Next I use my intuition to sense where on the body we should burn the kambo points. Traditionally, kambo is placed on either the inner ankle or the shoulder. The ankle placement offers a slower, more gradual medicine experience, which can be good for a first-timer, but shoulder treatments come on faster and pass quicker. The shoulder burns also seem to heal faster and scar less often.

Once we begin, I typically invite a first-timer to sit with just one point for a minute or two so that they can become comfortable with what is happening before we ramp up the potency. When it is time to add more medicine, I ask for consent. In this way, a sense of safety and comfort emerges, which empowers a person to relax enough to trust the medicine and open fully to its gifts.

Unfortunately, many people, especially on the Internet, seem to think that kambo must necessarily entail a harsh, brutish ordeal that borders on traumatic suffering. Quite honestly, I suspect that people are often being given unnecessarily large doses based on mental logic rather than intuitive guidance. Once, for instance, I had a client who is obese, and I was intuitively guided to give her just two points of medicine, which was more than sufficient for her to have a good purge, and she told me afterwards that she was grateful for how gentle it was, because her previous practitioner had given her a huge dose, perhaps based on thinking that her body size dictated it. But actually, sometimes large men need only a few points of the medicine, while other times, I have had thin, small-boned women who needed five or six points to throw up. I think what is too often disregarded is how essential it is to tune into the intuition in doing this work. People can become too mentally dominated and forget that, however physically medicinal the substance itself truly is, ultimately, this is a spirit medicine.

In my time as a kambo practitioner, I have seen kambo work many miracles. In fact, I have never witnessed a kambo ceremony that didn't bring about a remarkable transformation.

I have seen kambo help survivors of domestic abuse purge their pain and transform from downtrodden, depressed and hunch-shouldered to bright, cheerful, confident and empowered versions of themselves.

I watched people who struggled with chronic intestinal infections benefit from kambo's fungicidal properties, vomiting out gnarly masses of brown gunk from their intestines and getting dramatic relief from their symptoms right after.

I saw a woman who was sick with recurrent pneumonia recover after just one kambo treatment.

I saw a man who had nerve damage from chemotherapy report that sensation was returning to his fingers during his kambo ceremony, even though that had not been his goal. People often say they can feel the presence of the frog spirit moving around the body, looking for what needs healing and doctoring whatever it finds. (This is why placement of the medicine is not so important – it travels where it needs to go).

Another person, a silver-haired vegan lady, was surprised to notice that she felt the frog healing her spine during her ceremony, apparently repairing old injuries she had long forgotten about.

I saw kambo work a miracle on a man in his late sixties who could barely walk because of severe joint pain and other complications from Lyme disease. He had been bitten by a tick in Texas and suffered terribly for nearly forty years, despite trying every pharmaceutical approach the conventional doctors offered, some of which he said had brought pain worse than the disease itself. He had tried a number of herbal remedies, too. He was sedentary because moving around hurt. Yet after just one kambo treatment, he was up and about, stretching his arms and going for walks. Four treatments in, he reported that the inflammation had lessened by eighty percent. After seven, he told me he felt good as new, and soon he was hiking five miles a day with ease. Kambo restored his vitality.

I had clients who felt stuck in depression and anxiety, who were so unhappy that they were hardly eating or engaging with life, who after a few kambo treatments recovered their *joie de vivre*. The frog helped them to reclaim their sense of self, dust off what was once buried beneath the weight of emotional pain, and resume their forgotten passions and hobbies. They emerged from their treatments looking visibly lighter, brighter, and rejuvenated, and their friends and family noticed.

I watched heartbroken people who had lost loved ones and cherished relationships purge their grief in kambo ceremonies. I saw them pour out the tears and sadness that had gotten stuck in their bodies as phlegm into their buckets, and then emerge looking radiant and feeling serene, ready to move forward with their lives.

I have seen many people make major lifestyle changes for the better after getting a kambo treatment. They cut out junk food, they quit smoking, they gave up alcohol and started working out. This is not surprising. Kambo has a reputation for helping heal addictions of all kinds. It does so by detoxing the body, removing cravings, hitting the reset button neurochemically, and through spiritual cleansing. There are even now some clinics that give kambo to people who are kicking heroin and meth.

Kambo is good for so many things that it is easy to view it as a kind of panacea. And yet, it is also not for everybody. There are some marked contraindications: kambo is not safe for people with pregnancy, bipolar disorder, epilepsy, and heart conditions especially.

The frog sacrifices something to give up its secretions. While it does not die during a harvest, it is usually a stressful experience for the creature, and so kambo must not be used in vain. Of course, the medicine is in some ways its own deterrent, in that kambo can be harrowing to receive and those who seek it know that it requires some courage and willingness to endure discomfort. I have turned people away on a few occasions, when I sensed that the medicine would be too hard on them mentally or physically, or when I thought they were really needing an inner remedy instead. Even when someone is completely healthy, kambo is not always the right choice.

And, even when kambo has been good for someone, it doesn't mean that it is good to do perpetually, or indefinitely. There is such a thing as too much kambo. I know because I did it.

20

TOO MUCH KAMBO

Once I had my own supply of kambo, I treated myself regularly – a little too regularly, as it turned out. If you use the medicine when you do not need it physically or emotionally, I learned, it raises your vibration very high and can blast you into a heightened state of psychic awareness that lasts for a good week or two, with a powerful boost of extra physical energy, too. These qualities are the very same that make kambo popular among indigenous hunters in the Amazon rainforest who use it prior to tracking expeditions in the jungle.

I went for hours-long hikes, and as I did, the forest took on vivid colors. Everything looked like it was in high definition. I could feel the prana radiated by the trees and inhale it. I felt as though the ambient prana was animating me and powering my life force such that I was no longer running on the stored vital energy of my human body. I could perceive the spirits of the trees, and sense their different personalities, and when I communed with them by opening my heart, I easily received their teachings and wisdom.

I had visions of Archangel Metatron weaving new timelines of experiences and opportunities into my reality. I could visually see streams of white light in places where people did a lot of spiritual practices. I felt acutely aware of the illusion of the Self, the limitations of the human tendency to identify with past experiences and string up stories about them, and instead of a person, I began to view myself as a vessel through which angels and plants and animal spirits all shared their gifts, like I was a collage and also kind of a chimera.

Kambo isn't psychedelic in the sense that during a ceremony, one does not typically enter into an altered state, although it can make you lightheaded. But the effects it gives you afterwards can make the rest of your life feel pretty trippy. If you overdo it, as I did, it can give you an experience that is hard to distinguish from what might be called a manic state: you are amped up, have trouble sleeping and seem tense and wired like you're over-caffeinated. At one point I had a bad bout of insomnia that lasted for weeks. I was hardly sleeping and really out of it. I went to a park to ground myself, and I was walking barefoot on the grass in such a daze that people came over and asked if I was tripping. During this time I once tried to buy groceries but was so overwhelmed by being in a bustling store that I broke down and gave up the attempt. I ran outside and kicked off my shoes and climbed a gingko tree in the landscaping, and there I sat in the branches, feeling so extremely out of place in this civilization, and like a total weirdo. The psychic effects of kambo were designed for people living in nature, where amplifying one's sensitivity to the subtle energies happens in a fairly quiet and peaceful environment. Making oneself overly sensitive in an urban setting is madness.

The insomnia situation culminated in my going to the emergency room at a hospital and having to take pharmaceuticals to sleep, because even if I stacked my sedative herbs, I couldn't. So after that happened, I took a year off from using kambo and returned to it only when the frog omens called me back in undeniable ways – and even then, very sparingly.

In the years since, I've learned to dialogue directly with my spirit guides if I'm unsure about whether it's time. I'll say, "If it's for my highest good to use kambo right now, please show me some clear signs. My mind thinks it's a good idea but I would like some very obvious confirmation before I do it." One of the last times I said that, I walked into a restaurant and saw a frog in the decor inside, and then I went into a gift shop where I saw five frog figurines for sale. Another time right after I said it, I happened to be watching a Sandra Bullock movie and her character had this strange tangential dialogue about tree frogs.

The Universe is an intelligent field, and Spirit is always listening.

21

MAGIC TREES

There are two particular Douglas Fir trees planted across from each other in Portland's Laurelhurst Park, near the pond, that are special. They emanate a beautifully soft, gentle energy of loving kindness, and when you sit there, all the stresses of life disappear and you just want to *be* there for as long as you can, soaking up the peace.

I found these trees one day in the summer, and I returned every day to commune with their magic once I did.

I wasn't the only one who could feel it.

There was a guy who set up a huge gong and a set of crystal singing bowls in front of them and offered free healings to passersby. "It's a selfish thing," he said, "Because everybody is me in a different body. I'm just helping myself."

At night he guided people through secret ceremonies with DMT and psilocybin there, because that was what had lit him up. He was an entrepreneur who was visiting the city for the summer and he slept in a van parked on the edge of the park, so he could focus all his energy on helping others.

He attracted a tribe of supportive friends around him, who brought him gifts of food and weed and musical instruments to play. People would come and go throughout the day, have deep conversations, meditate together and just hang out. It was a lot of fun.

There was one person in this group who I felt particularly drawn to. We tended to sit across from each other under the trees at the same time every day, even though we never planned it.

Those DMT trips changed his life. He left his wife and children, quit his well-paying job and gave away most of his possessions, because he felt they would distract him from pursuing the spiritual path completely. He was always either meditating, making art, or doing acts of service. Whenever he had money, he'd give it away.

He gave up eating for a little while, and sleeping, too.

"You have to eat and sleep," I told him.

"I'm so connected to my soul that I don't think I need to," he said.

"You do need to," I insisted. "Your body needs to be nourished so that your soul can live in it."

Sometimes I'd see him wandering around the park barefoot and shirtless, looking a little bit dazed. Just like I once had. As he walked around looking kind of out of it, but very happy, I sometimes held his hand, both because it felt good and because in his hyper-awakened state, it seemed like he might just float up into the sky.

I felt tremendous love and affection for him, in a platonic sort of way. He felt like a member of my soul family, a kindred spirit, a person I knew deeply even though we had only just met, a brother.

We had a great time walking around together and connecting with the trees. We could both tune into the specific energies and spirits inside them. It was a joyful thing.

One day he looked into my eyes and he said, "I know who you are."

"Oh? Who do you think I am?" I replied.

"I know you're Green Tara," he said, pointedly.

"And how did you come to that conclusion?" I asked.

"The tree told me," he said. "It also showed me that in a past life I was Gautama, the buddha, and I started to remember."

22

MEETING GOD

The last time I attended an ayahuasca ceremony, it was by divine invitation. I hadn't sought it out at all. At least, not consciously.

Each morning, I lit a mapacho cigarette and inhaled the feeling of loving kindness into my heart, where I held a prayer for an end to suffering for all beings and a great healing for the Earth, and then I exhaled the smoke into a dreamcatcher I had made, intending the web to be like a mandala, a symbol for the interconnectedness of all beings – a cosmic web, if you will. I intended this to be a powerful ritual, but I had no idea that it would invite replies, nor how much would transpire from it.

A barrage of invitations suddenly arrived to attend ayahuasca ceremonies, and they began streaming in at the rate of literally every other day. I got phone calls, I got emails, I got invited in person, and once, even while checking out at a grocery store, a cashier noticed the kambo scars on my arm and told me about an upcoming ayahuasca ceremony!

At the same time, I started to feel an inner alarm bell going off, pushing me to become more conscious of my thoughts, resolve any interpersonal resentments I still held toward anybody, and elevate myself into a relentlessly positive frame of mind. I gave myself a kambo treatment and restarted my meditation practice with gusto. I felt a burning desire to do acts of service every day, to help everyone around me in whatever way I could.

I felt a strong call to clean up my diet[7] to help my physical body better resonate with the subtle, high vibrational energies of the divine realms, as well. The body is an instrument, a vessel for the soul, and when that instrument is clogged, the intuition can become very foggy – as can the mind. Eating healthier, whole, unprocessed food makes a tremendous difference. I also did a four-day water fast to detoxify myself and further raise my frequency.

Meanwhile, I waited until one of the ayahuasca ceremony invitations I received resonated in my heart as a strong "Yes." This one came from Hummingbird, the woman who had supported me in a previous ceremony years before, the one in which I had gone through a death and rebirth process.

Hummingbird told me that this ceremony was going to be very special. She often visited the Amazon jungle to drink ayahuasca with indigenous shamans she respected, and she said that a group of women shamans she knew from these trips to the Amazon jungle had come to her in a dream and told her to hold this ceremony. Hummingbird wanted her first ceremony as head facilitator to be a celebration of the divine feminine, and so she invited only women

---

[7] Diet is a very personal thing, and what is most healthy and supportive for one individual can be totally inappropriate for another. Our constitutions vary so much, based on genetics and the particular needs and challenges of our bodies. If you read my first book, *Dandelion Hunter*, you might recall that I wrote about being vegetarian for sixteen years. No longer. I eventually discovered that that diet did not leave my body physically healthy even though I loved the concept of it. When it came to a crisis point and I realized I had to make a change, I was intuitively guided to follow a very clean, low-carbohydrate paleo diet with plenty of wild fish and grass-fed, humanely raised meat. This was a tricky thing for me to accept and I tried many times to go back to vegetarianism unsuccessfully. When I recently read the Dalai Lama's autobiography, I was relieved to learn that he went through the same experience. He tried to be vegetarian when he moved to India, but it made his body unhealthy, so he couldn't sustain it. Meat eating is part of Tibetan Buddhist life, even as they try their best to embody *ahimsa*, respect for all living beings, and nonviolence.

to participate, and hand-picked every person. Each of us would be welcome to bring musical instruments and contribute, which was also special; in my previous experiences, only the shamans running the ceremony sang, unless it was the very end of the work and everyone was celebrating. I felt honored to be invited and I began practicing *icaros* to share.

Hummingbird's ceremony was held in the comfortable, lushly carpeted living room of a participant's home in a rural setting. The space had a very high, two-story ceiling. The group was made up of about ten people who all knew each other from previous ceremonies. Most of us had driven long distances to get there and everyone was in buoyant spirits; we were excited to make music together and excited to support Hummingbird in her first time being a facilitator.

Instead of the austere tone that accompanied the other ceremonies I have been to, Hummingbird's had a celebratory, festive feeling to it. I took my seat and waited to see what would unfold.

The medicine brought on a vision like a little animated movie in my mind, a procession of images accompanied by claircognizant understandings. I saw God pluck me from a golden realm that was my home – a place filled with golden light and higher consciousness – and send me down to Planet Earth on a mission. I was shown that on Earth many people feel lost, confused and disconnected, much to His chagrin. He then showed me a radio tower broadcasting across the world, and indicated that this tower represented me.

When I opened my eyes again and looked up, I saw a cartoon-like overlay floating above the group of people in the room. Just beneath the second-story ceiling there was a great big dais on a cloud, upon which God Himself, the divine father, was seated. He looked a bit like a Greek philosopher. He wore a white robe, had a gray beard, and an arm outstretched towards me. He reached down from those Heavenly clouds and bestowed upon me a fleet of white horses and a golden throne – His own Army, the Forces of Heaven.

I could hardly believe what I was seeing.

Next a vortex opened beside the divine father. It was a space-time portal, next to which a group of loving beings had gathered to send gifts. They looked like a very diverse array of kind souls from across the universe. There were people dressed in rope sandals from other ages, dark-skinned people wearing indigenous clothing, and even non-human looking individuals who looked like they had come from galaxies far away. I sensed that these were all beings who had heard my mapacho prayers carried by the smoke into the cosmic web, and in their hands they held magical gourds containing vibrational blessings and blueprints for a better world that they were going to pour through the portal.

Was this going to bring an end to suffering on Earth? Was *I* really going to be part of this moment? *Madre* Ayahuasca replied to my thoughts by waving a little cartoon banner across my eyes that said, "BELIEVE IN YOURSELF."

I could not believe it. I was beyond overwhelmed. Was this really happening? My eyes went wide and my jaw dropped. I could hardly process that it was real. The shock of it all overwhelmed me and unfortunately, something inside me began to panic intensely.

Deep down I felt unworthy of being in God's presence and taking part in such a profound and epic moment. My mind started whirring with anxiety and I suddenly started feeling my life's regrets and thinking of times I felt like I had fallen short of my ideals. As my mental and emotional vibrations dropped, my consciousness moved into ego and out of oneness. I saw the vortex wane and begin to disintegrate, and I heard a male voice on the dais exclaim with horror, "You're polluting!"

I began to feel absolute panic. Had I just ruined everything?

God spoke. He said, "Listen to your sisters!" and I sensed He was aiming to redirect my attention away from my thoughts by bringing me into the present moment. The other women in the room were singing beautiful songs and melodies. It felt like a celebration. As I looked around, colorful patterns danced in the air before my eyes and their voices were weaving a new reality into the fabric of space-time, infusing Earth's future with threads of peace, joy and love. I was glad to see it.

But, had I screwed up my part? What about the vortex? What about the blessings from those otherworldly beings who were about to pour their magical gifts through the portal that disintegrated? I wasn't sure, but I had a horrible feeling that I had messed up, and I began to feel immense shame.

God spoke to me once more before the ceremony came to a close. He said to me with a sigh, "There will *be* other opportunities."

He added, "Heal the world with your voice."

Still, I was distraught, and after the ceremony ended, I sought Hummingbird's counsel about what had happened.

"How can you 'screw up' if everything that happens is perfect?" she said.

"But how could *that* be perfect?" I asked her.

What merit was I supposed to glean from the series of events that had just transpired? How could I feel good about something that felt like failure? And Hummingbird said: "Self-love."

She helped me understand that the sense of unworthiness that had arisen within me and lowered my frequency during the ceremony, disconnecting me from resonating with Heaven, had been a symptom of self-judgment and self-criticism. It was perfectionism run amok. It was a sign that I had more work to do in my spiritual evolution before I was ready to be of service on the level I wanted to be. We might think that on the spiritual path, resonating with unconditional love is just about loving and accepting other people, but it's just as much about coming to peace with our own selves, and all we have done in our lives, including our missteps.

"Ego takes up space where self-love isn't," Hummingbird said.

So that became my next curriculum: to master self-love.

I attended Hummingbird's next ceremony a month later, hoping that with more positive thinking I could stay in oneness consciousness that time and make up for what I viewed as kind of a flub. I saw the divine dais materialize once again with the Divine Father upon it. When I saw Him, I apologized for how things went last time – for dropping my vibration in the midst of the weaving of a new world blueprint – and I asked for His forgiveness.

To my surprise, God laughed. "Forgive *yourself*, Tara," He said.

PART II: INITIATIONS INTO POWER

23

WANDERING

It took me a very long time to recover from feeling as though I had possibly failed the world. I became very depressed and unsure of myself, and I lost the will to do my work. This made a lot of things very difficult, including my finances. I had been staying with a good friend for free, but right after that ceremony, in the winter of 2019, she needed her spare room back so that her ailing mother could visit, and I quickly found myself with nowhere to go, with very little money.

I thought I was heading into an awkward but brief transition period of couch surfing until things sorted themselves out. That is not what happened. What happened was that I was homeless for the better part of that year, and depending how you look at it, quite a bit longer, too.

For the first three months, I couchsurfed with friends. It was nice to spend time with people I loved, but it was also tricky because as an introvert and former homebody, it was really difficult to ground and center myself while crashing in someone's living room, and perpetually on the move.

In order to create a sense of stability, I created a daily routine that made life feel consistent despite the fact that everything was always uncertain and up in the air. Exercise was a real stress-reliever.

I went jogging every morning, lifted weights in the gym every day after that, and listened to guided mindfulness meditations first thing in the morning, again in the afternoon, and the longest right before bed, when I felt naturally relaxed. I took anti-anxiety herbs every day to keep myself feeling calm, especially lemon balm, kava kava and passionflower. I coped pretty well by doing all this, and eventually my spirits picked up again – as much as they could under the circumstances – and things improved. I once again began seeing clients for kambo, intuitive healing, and spiritual counseling.

Yet, even with some good money coming in again, I could not find a place to land. The rising cost of Portland apartments were now out of reach for my income, and with a huge influx of newcomers to the city, the population was booming and room rentals were in short supply – and those that were dog friendly were even harder to find. The few opportunities that seemed like a possible fit for me somehow disappeared as quickly as I found them. It was disheartening.

As the months wore on and there were no more friends to stay with, I asked for help from my broader community on social media. This was very humbling and vulnerable to do, but I could see no other option.

I steeled myself by listening to angelic healing meditations every day, especially one narrated by Kim Caldwell about calling upon Archangel Gabriel to bless you with miracles in seemingly hopeless situations. Well, this very much worked. Not only did I feel strengthened and aligned by this practice, but a Facebook friend who I had never met messaged me out of the blue, saying that she felt spiritually called to invite me to stay for a little while with her family – in an apartment that happened to be in Southwest Portland, located right next to Gabriel Park!

This place was really a boon. They even gave me my own bedroom to stay in. I felt optimistic again, and like things were going to work out for me after all. But after two weeks, the couple had a huge fight and decided that they needed to separate imminently, and so they needed their spare room back right away for one of them to sleep in. Once again I didn't know where to go or what to do, but I tried not to worry. I listened to my angel meditations dutifully and tried my best to believe that something would work out.

It did. I got a text from a kambo client spontaneously asking if I'd like to house-sit her apartment for the next two weeks -- and it was a paying gig, too. This magical, miraculous turn of events coming at the most perfect time amazed me. It was actually an upgrade, because it meant I got some actual solitude in a rural setting for the next two weeks. Those two weeks were like a retreat for me and I began to truly elevate into a place of deep peace and connection to my Higher Self. Things were really looking like they were on the upswing again, and I felt optimistic. But at the end of the gig, I was once again without a home, and this time, a new door didn't open.

But I did have some money, so I rented Air BnBs and motel rooms, sometimes moving every two days. It was extremely stressful – and quite expensive. When my funds dried up again, I had to get really creative.

There was a night when I rolled out my sleeping bag in the backyard of a healer colleague who lived in a sketchy neighborhood with a chain-link fence around her yard. She said that was the best she could offer; I wasn't invited to stay indoors because someone she lived with was allergic to dogs, and Daisy was with me. "Well," I thought, "At least I have her as a protector. She is a good watchdog." That ounce of positive attitude I could muster dissipated the next morning when I woke up on the grass to find that Daisy had gotten sprayed by a skunk.

"Well now we've done it, Universe," I thought. "I guess we've found my rock bottom."

So this was what life had come to? All my spiritual efforts had amounted to...this? It all seemed so pointless, so I drowned my sorrows in a gallon of ice cream – to which I am mildly allergic, but in such a situation of deep despair, seemed not to matter anymore. What did I care if my face swelled up and my intestines bloated? Just then, I got a text message. An acquaintance I had met at a community campout a month before wanted to know if I was still between places, and said that if I was, he wanted to offer me a spare room to stay in for a couple weeks. And I thought, "Wow. Here comes another act of grace in the exact right moment." He was very generous. He gave me his spare room, left me money for laundry, and handed me three hundred dollars cash as a gift, too. I stayed there for a little more than two weeks, until his romantic aspirations towards me became a problem, so I had to move – again.

There were so many ups and downs like this. That year was a roller coaster. It was very wearying, and very difficult. It was hard to accept the lack of control I had over my life. I often felt frustrated, sad, confused and overwhelmed. But I also discovered that it was possible to accept the situation and surrender to the intense uncertainty and vulnerability it entailed, because my faith was strong, synchronicities abounded and I could often sense a divine hand orchestrating things.

Everywhere I went, there were little omens – little symbolic messages appearing that seemed sent from above and which guided me through this ordeal. For example, in one motel room where I stayed for a few nights, there was a flamingo motif in the landscaping. I knew that flamingos represent transition, a time of being in-between places in one's life – and so that felt appropriate and even humorous, as if the cosmic mirror was reflecting an acknowledgement of my station in life, and assuring me that it was temporary.

At an AirBnB room I rented, there were fabric tulips sitting in a vase on a dresser. This was meaningful because I had recently purchased a bouquet of tulips and placed them with a thank-you card on an altar as an offering of gratitude to my guides and angels for their help. It was like they were winking back at me.

When I stayed with the couple that broke up, I found myself in a housing development curiously called Shadow Hills, and while I stayed there I found my consciousness being directed inwards to do some deep introspection about the painful spaces of my psyche in which I needed to forgive myself, which is exactly the sort of thing a Jungian psychologist might call doing "shadow work."

When I was couchsurfing with friends who had a young child, I noticed unicorn emblems were everywhere, from the decor to the cartoons on the TV to the toys strewn about, and this was meaningful, too, because unicorns are a symbol of wonderful magical things, of the impossible becoming possible, and also of unconditional love, which is the vibrational frequency of the Kingdom of Heaven. In mythic stories, unicorns appear only to very gentle people who have pure, loving hearts worthy of their trust (traditionally, only young women). This was a sweet signpost my guides were setting before me, to remind me to stay lighthearted and trust in divine miracles.

Eventually I came to suspect that the difficult circumstances before me were actually meant to be there, and that it was not an accident nor even a misfortune that I was wandering around like this. I sensed that I was being put through this hardship so that I could evolve through it. It was like a sort of boot camp, one *intended* to stress me out, break down my ego and forge a new consciousness steeped in faith.

Of course, it was still excruciating at times. I often felt as though I was going to fall apart from all the pressure and uncertainty of my situation – unless I pulled all of my awareness into the present moment. If it was a day when I did not know where I would be sleeping at night and I had no money, then only in the present moment, only in that one particular minute, feeling the weight of my body on a surface, breathing clean air, and noticing that my belly was full, was life manageable. The next moment did not yet exist – the one in which it seemed like there was no plan, no backup, no net, no resources – so as long as I just stayed *right here*, I was okay. Even if I was feeling anxious in the present moment, I learned that I was safe, and it was okay feeling anxious. It would pass.

And if I stayed just in *this moment,* and ignored all thoughts of the next moment, often I noticed that life felt quite good. I remember one morning in particular I awoke in a really nice AirBnb room with plush bedding and soft carpets beneath my feet. The shared bathroom had a soaking tub in it, and the common room had a really nice white leather couch. I sat on the couch and focused on how the cushions gave me a comforting sense of being supported. As I dwelled on that positive, nourishing feeling, I received a text from a stranger asking if she could book multiple kambo ceremonies. She sent me a generous sum of money electronically right away, as a donation to secure our appointment for the work. It appeared that I had raised my frequency up very high in positive energy and a feeling of abundance, and in so doing, had attracted the circumstances that matched and mirrored the emotional feeling I had generated of safety, support and stability. It had insta-manifested.

When I was focusing on positive energy and the grace that was everywhere around me, life felt very blessed and magical, and prosperity flowed abundantly.

But on the days when I didn't do that, when I felt frustrated at the lack of control I had over my life, or when I listened to the anxious voice inside who told sad stories about my situation and called it hopeless and scary, then it all felt very heavy and depressing and hard to bear, and money was nowhere to be found. The contrast was stark.

Although it was very clear what I had to do, I did resist at times. I did not like the idea of having to sit passively, like an undulating piece of coral waiting for plankton to float by in the ocean current in order to eat. Sometimes, I really just wanted to be the shark and feel a sense of control by taking action, like people who have conventional jobs and conventional lives. There was a battle inside myself about this. For instance, I tried taking the initiative to market my work and contact potential clients instead of magnetizing them passively and quietly, attracting work in divine timing. On one such day when my ego was flexing, I got distracted and crashed my beloved car, a shimmering champagne pink 2013 Chevy Spark with an antenna that looked like a unicorn horn. Sparkles bit the dust under very unusual circumstances: I rear-ended a tow truck at barely thirty miles an hour. The truck was fine. It had not even a scratch on it, yet this low-impact tap completely totalled my ride. There it went, my sole property. No one was hurt except me. I emerged with a bloody nose and a bruise mysteriously shaped exactly like an arrow pointing to the left, on my left knee. In spirit medicine, the left side of the body is considered the yin side, and it is associated with surrender, receiving, and connection to divine guidance. The knee symbolizes moving forward. This was a strong message. Heaven was saying, "Sit still. Attract. Magnetize. And if you don't, I'll beat you down until it is not a choice." The crash was no accident.

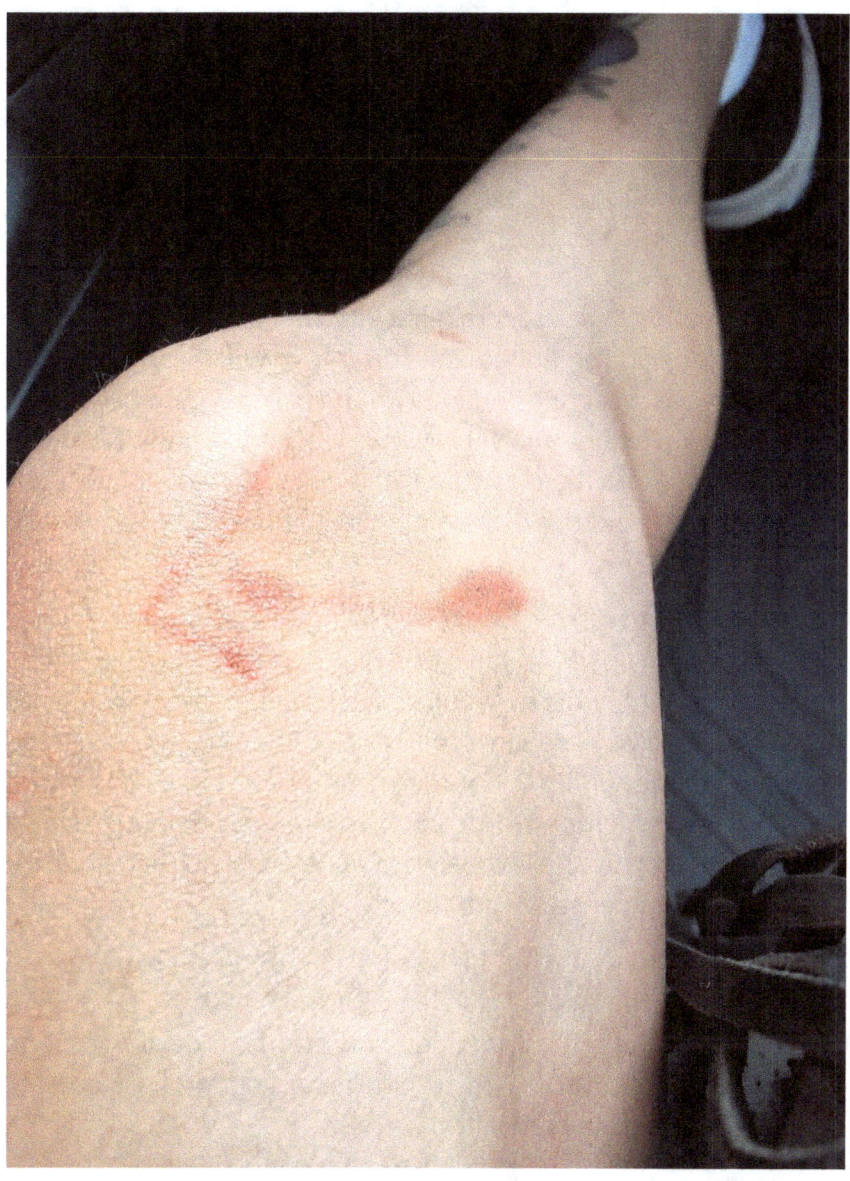

With my car now kaput, I rode my bicycle all over the city. This was fine for the summer. It was less fine in the autumn, when it was getting very cold and rainy. Fortunately, a kind friend in the plant medicine community generously loaned me his spare Toyota

Prius to drive. Because it was the only constant as I moved around from motel room to motel room around the chilly city now, the car began to feel like a bit of a home to me.

One night, as I opened the door to yet another AirBnb rental, I sighed. It was thick with a heavy residue of the emotions left by the visitors before me. It felt very dirty with negative energy. I was too tired to try and clean it, and sad for myself. So I gave up. I got into the car and drove to Laurelhurst Park, the place with the magic trees where I had meditated comfortably many days, and there I slept in the backseat of the Toyota Prius in my sleeping bag. It was cold, January weather, and yet I awoke with a smile and a feeling of peace. Moving into the car actually felt *good*, so that's what I did. I craved stability, and this offered it, despite how unconventional it was.

I was surprised to discover how well living in a car worked for me. I'd wake up at the park, go for a jog around the perimeter, and then drive to the gym, where I would exercise and then shower, and then I would go buy prepared food to eat. After that I'd drive to do my work as a healer or I'd visit friends and have fun. And the best part was, I never had to worry about where I was going to sleep. I was like a turtle; my shell was always right there, no matter where I went. I took immense comfort in this.

Sadly, my friend asked for his car back, and then I really found myself back in the chaos again, and this time with no car *and* no place to live. One night I was sleeping on the floor of my friend Johnananda's backyard shed-turned-recording-studio. He could only spare it for a couple nights.

"Johnananda, I'm so stressed out and I don't know what to do. It seems like whenever I get on my feet, the bottom drops out beneath me. My life isn't making sense," I said.

"Have you thought about leaving Portland?" he asked.

"No, actually I haven't," I said.

But then I began to wonder: Had I lost resonance with Portland? Was that what was happening? Was it all falling apart because I was being divinely re-routed?

Certainly the city had changed in the years I spent there. When I arrived in 2008 it was a quirky, laid-back bohemian paradise where people walked goats on leashes down the street and I foraged wild herbs in overgrown lots. Now "Hub City" was a bustling, gentrified metropolis filled with luxury high-rises and traffic jams.

"There's not enough nature here for you anymore," Johnananda said. "There is nowhere for you to set down your roots. You can't ground."

"That seems true," I said.

"Your guides are showing me that you have limited yourself to this place; it looks like you've been wearing a ball and chain around your ankle," he said.

"You're right," I said, "but I don't know where else to go. Do you have any intuitive hits?"

"Let me see," Johnananda said. He closed his eyes and smiled. "Have you thought about the Southwest?"

"Hmm. I sure do love the sun," I said. "That sounds pretty good."

"First, try Eugene," he said. "And go to the ocean."

I respected Johnananda's guidance greatly because I knew that he was not just a fellow Reiki master but also a very advanced spiritual adept along the path of kriya yoga. He goes to India to visit his guru in an ashram, and when he is apart from his teacher he speaks with him telepathically. He is also a disciple of the great kriya yoga master Paramahamsa Yogananda, author of the very inspiring, miracle-filled book *Autobiography of a Yogi*, with whom Johnananda has a vivid connection.

I set out to follow his instructions very literally. I used a phone app to find a rental car in town. I got myself a minivan for thirty dollars a night, and I decided it would be my new home. I took what few possessions I had left in it and I drove directly to Eugene, where I visited a friend who needed a kambo treatment. But I didn't stay in Eugene long because it didn't feel like home. Instead I filled up my gas tank and drove directly west on Route 126 for just over an hour, until I saw signs for the ocean.

And that's how I "accidentally" found myself living in a van at the ocean in a town locals call The Flor-Tex, because it is a magical place that has a way of sucking you in.

24

ENTERING THE FLOR-TEX

It was midnight when I pulled into the parking lot of a 7-Eleven convenience store in the coastal town of Florence, Oregon. I stopped in to ask for directions to the beach. I didn't care that it was very late at night. I had driven a long way and I wanted to see those waves crashing on the sand as soon as I could.

The clerk told me it was a simple route, just a couple of turns and I'd be right there.

As I walked back to my car from the store, I noticed that, in the space next to mine, someone had parked a dark green Chevy G20 van plastered with colorful, witty bumper stickers and shimmering crystals glued to the dashboard.

"I like that person," I thought. A tall, pretty brunette woman about my age exited the store just then and leaned against the van door.

"I like your van," I told her.

"Thanks," she said.

"Do you live in it?" I asked.

"Sometimes I live in it when my old man kicks me out," she said.

"Fuck him, man. That's shitty," I said.

"Yeah," she said. "Do you want to see it?"

139

I did. I was very curious what the interior would look like. She pulled the side door open and gave me the tour. She had a bed in the back, and lots of clothing on hangers. Cargo nets were strung up across the walls, holding things. There was a big comfy chair to sit in. And my favorite feature was the stick-on glow-in-the-dark stars glowing on the ceiling. It looked like a portable bedroom, and it looked spacious enough to do yoga inside.

"Wow, that is so cool. I'm living in this minivan," I said, pointing to my all-black Honda Odyssey. "It's a rental."

There wasn't much to see in there, but at least I had a home. I had taken the back seats out to make room for a foam pad, which I topped with a pillow and a sleeping bag. On the floor I had a duffel bag of my clothing and a reusable shopping bag holding my toiletries next to it, some books and my drum and kambo medicine bag. The minivan's best features were its heated black leather seats and one of those hang down mini-screens in the back on which I could watch DVDs.

"Someday I'd love to have something like yours," I told her.

"You will," she said.

We said goodbye and I drove five minutes to the sea, where I parked the car and announced to my dog Daisy, "We made it to the ocean! Let's go see the waves!" I flung open the door and the two of us ran up the sand dunes and down to the water under the stars, feeling joyful and free. It was magnificent. I felt happy for the first time in a long time, like a little kid again.

25

SPARROW

In the morning I awoke around sunrise and started the engine so that I could have some heat. It was the end of February and the Oregon coast is chilly in the winter and spring. The morning temperatures are in the thirties (Fahrenheit) and the daytime highs are in the low fifties. I turned on the radio to the jazz station, stretched and put on a hat, gloves, and warm jacket so that I could take a long morning walk across the white-sand beach. The sky was overcast and gray, yet I felt cheerful. Everywhere I looked, there was beauty. I walked for hours, and while I did, I could feel the salty sea breeze cleansing my auric field, sweeping away all the stress of life in the city and filling me up with good vibes. I was so glad to be in nature, and I felt wonderfully peaceful and calm.[8]

When the sun came out the day warmed and I took off my shoes and placed them barefoot on the sand. As I did, I could feel my nervous system grounding as electricity flowed out through the soles of my feet. I laid down on the beach on my belly and made a pillow of my hands and I felt this effect even more. My body relaxed, and I could sense the gentle love of Mother Nature radiating from the ground. I could feel her healing energy flowing in and out of my

---

[8]   A 2006 study published in the *American Journal of Psychiatry* found that high-density negative air ionization had a similar effect to sunlight in terms of easing depression, which helps the body produce serotonin and ease seasonal sadness.

chakras, as She balanced and rejuvenated them. It was so soothing. I felt like a small child being held safely and lovingly by her mother.

When I rose again I ate a lunch of cucumbers and avocados that I had in a cooler and then I collected seashells and colored them with markers to entertain myself. In the afternoon I found there was a little forest of rhododendrons and Douglas fir trees lining the sand dunes with hiking trails running through them. I felt I had found a little slice of Paradise. It was an easy decision to declare this park my new home. Sure, there were signs that said "no overnight camping," but that was a rule for people with options.

I was comfortable with stealth. I moved my parking spot daily to give the appearance of being someone who simply came early and stayed late. Eventually I could tell the park rangers were suspicious, but I was very friendly to them and they had warm hearts, so they looked the other way. All they really cared about, they told me, was that no one littered. They were nature lovers who wanted to use their power and authority to protect the beach and make it a safe place for the public. They were not there to harass anybody. I was very fortunate that was the case, because only a couple of weeks into my stay there, the world went bananas with the Covid-19 outbreak and the pandemic pandemonium caused a sudden government-mandated "quarantine," a shut-down of society. Now I really had nowhere else to go.

The officials actually shut down every coastal park in Oregon – except for the one I happened to find myself living in. It was allowed to stay open by the grace of a technicality – perhaps because it included the Siuslaw River within its boundaries, it was controlled by the regional government instead of by the state, so the governor didn't have the jurisdiction to close it, and the ranger in charge of that park was determined to keep it open. He understood the healing power of nature, and he wanted the public to have access to its beauty, especially in this time of great stress and uncertainty.

Although I was very much isolated and alone, I did not feel lonely, because the presence of Mother Nature was everywhere around me, and I could even sense *Madre* herself in all of it. Hummingbirds and dragonflies flitted about, dazzling with their bright iridescence of turquoise and fuchsia and indigo blue. The gentle roar of the ocean became the calming soundtrack to my existence. The positive vibes and negative ions emitted by the rolling waves infused my spirit with peace and happiness. I could feel the happy prana radiated by the stately rhododendron trees lining the sand. And in every moment, I could count on the devoted companionship of my adorable best friend, Daisy, who was always up for a long walk or a rest on the sand. It was, in many ways, an idyllic existence.

I settled into a daily routine: long morning walks on the beach, working by phone as a transformational life coach and intuitive healer, or recording interviews with experts on entheogens for new episodes of my *Green Goddess* podcast. Then I would buy lunch at a local grocery store and drive to a majestic seaside overlook spot on the highway for the afternoon. There I ate while listening to 106.9 FM - KCST, a local radio station that plays an eclectic mix of "adult contemporary," classic rock (The Eagles, America, Fleetwood Mac), and Nineties alternative rock (Gin Blossoms, Cranberries, Nirvana). After lunch I'd make art, drawing flowers and other things that caught my eye, and sometimes do a little yoga in the van. Then I'd head back to the park and go for a sunset hike, and close the day by reading a novel before tucking in for the evening. Sometimes I rented DVD movies from the local Redbox vending machine at the 7-Eleven (always comedies) and watched them on the little screen in the minivan, too. Then, I fell asleep listening to guided meditations.

It all amounted to a nice life, and I felt very happy, and actually far happier than I had ever been in Portland, even with such Spartan accommodations as a bucket for a bathroom and a sleeping bag for a bed.

One day, on one of my long walks in the trees, I spotted that green Chevy van from the 7-Eleven, the one with all the stickers and crystals on it, parked at a trailhead. That tall brunette woman I had met on my first night in Florence was walking beside it, wandering around with her eyes fixed to the ground.

"Hey," I said to her.

She looked up at me for a moment, a little bit surprised to be jostled out of her trance and unsure who I was.

"We met at the 7-Eleven," I reminded her.

"Oh yeah," she said. "How's it going?"

"Good. I'm living here now," I said. "What are you doing? Foraging something?"

"Hunting for rocks," she said.

"Oh, like crystals?" I asked.

"Yeah," she said.

We got to talking more and then she said, "Hey, do you need a shower? I know showers are like gold when you live in a van. You can shower at my place."

"I've been getting by with baby wipes but that's probably a good idea some time. Where do you live?" I asked.

She wrote down her phone number and address on a piece of paper and handed it to me.

"When should I come by?" I asked.

"Whenever you want," she said.

I had been surprised that she didn't need me to call first or anything, but I showed up a few days later and had a wonderful hot shower, and she invited me to linger and enjoy the feeling of sitting on a couch again. I noticed that she had rose emblems and rose patterns all over the quaint one-story house. I cleaned her kitchen for her, to return the favor. This exchange became the beginning of a very sweet friendship between us, and I dropped by often. She wasn't always home, but I tried to do a little something each time to make her life easier, like wash her dishes, and she liked to leave me little gifts, trinkets such as a stuffed frog and a frog figurine, and goodies for Daisy, such as a bright yellow doggy rainjacket.

As we got to know each other, my new friend, whom I'll call Sparrow, told me that she was originally from Alaska, had gone to nursing school, and now made her living as a professional mushroom forager. (She is an adept herbalist, too). There was a tremendous abundance of fungi on the Oregon coast for her to pick – chanterelles, morels, oysters, lobsters, and such – and she knew all the very best spots. She had big bags of dried mushrooms in her pantry and she liked to send me off with them.

Sometimes I came by and she had friends hanging around. Many of them were living in their cars like I was, and some just drifted around without even a vehicle, so all kinds of people were often showering there or cooking and doing laundry. Some were young like us, some were elderly. Her place was kind of like a community shelter. Sometimes the house didn't have electricity or running water because Sparrow didn't have the money to pay the bills, so her friends gave her money whenever they could. Everyone pitched in. I'd see people gardening for her and doing little repair projects around the house, or collaborating with her on her paintings and music. She smoked cigarettes and played guitar and sang. It was a very playful environment. Sometimes she set up a tent in her backyard for me to sleep in, complete with an air mattress and a portable heater for the chilly nights, and she'd invite me to crash for days, and I did. It was really fun, and I'd bake cupcakes for her and her friends and decorate them with bright blue frosting, even though I didn't eat them, just because.

Sparrow loved to help people. She'd often have a big bag of donated clothing she'd foraged from the local thrift store. The shop was closed for the pandemic but people hadn't stopped dropping off their stuff, so she swooped in, gathered piles of it in big plastic trash bags and brought it home to give away to her friends. We all sorted through it and grabbed the gems we liked most. Once she even gave me a peridot and diamond necklace.

"You're like a fairy godmother," I told her.

"I like to bedazzle," she said. She meant that she liked to beautify the world, to leave people and things better than she found them. It was like a game to her, because she had so many different skills with which to do this. Not only was she a trained nurse, a forager, an herbalist, and a talented visual artist, she was also adept at fixing mechanical things, from cars to appliances, and she could sew clothing, too. Her resourcefulness is breathtaking. I have never seen anything like it.

"You're a MacGuyver," I told her.

"No, I'm a *Miss*Guyver," she quipped.

Sparrow also seemed to have endless energy. It took me a little while to catch on, but eventually I discovered that there was a reason: Meth.

What tipped me off was that sometimes she seemed like her cheerful, friendly self and other times she had an irritable, edgy, hyper-focused energy running through her that she channeled into house-cleaning binges and art projects on good days, but that on bad days, led to dramatic mood swings, sudden outbursts and angry fights with her boyfriend. She didn't think I knew she was using meth, but at a certain point it became obvious. I didn't confront her about it directly, because I knew she wanted it to be a secret, but when I sensed that she knew that I knew, I said, "I'm not judging you. Everyone has vices."

"It helps my ADHD," she said. I hadn't known that doctors actually prescribe a pharmaceutical concoction that is nearly identical to meth as treatment for ADHD, but it's true – they really do –

and Sparrow considered her approach to be a thrifty means to self-medicating.

All of her friends there apparently also had ADHD and were self-medicating. They generally seemed very cheerful and sweet and channeled their energy into art or productive fixer-upper projects. (Sparrow once said to me, "Don't trust a tweaker with a dirty house, because that means something is *seriously* wrong"). Yet the dark side was there, too. In her negative moods, which could come out of nowhere, Sparrow was prone to abruptly kicking everybody out of the house. Sometimes that was everybody except me, and sometimes it included me, too. When it did, she'd exclaim, "This is a drug house! You don't belong here!"

In some ways, it really was a drug house. I saw a couple of people in bad shape, suffering from the classic signs of meth addiction, like paranoia, rotting teeth and sores on their faces. They came to Sparrow's house for help with their ailments, knowing she wouldn't judge them. I watched her disinfect an oozing wound on an elderly woman's scalp, listen to her tales of woe, and treat her with dignity, never asking anything in return.

Sparrow's house was a port in the storm.

26

DEMONS

So much of modern life is an assault on the senses. The loud clanging of car doors, the roar of car engines as they accelerate, the frenzied hustle and bustle of people running their errands as quickly as they can, the fumes in the air – it is all in such stark contrast to the peaceful, quiet spaciousness of life in nature.

This was something I had to brace myself to handle whenever I needed to go get groceries. While on the one hand interacting with human civilization was kind of a refreshing counterbalance to my extreme solitude, it also felt harsh and overwhelming. As I walked around the stores, I noticed the static energy fields generated by electronic devices and the sterile, dead feeling of the air indoors. I could also feel the debris of negative emotions swimming around.

This was especially intense because it was the beginning of Covid lockdown, and people were feeling quite freaked out and worried when they shopped. Most wore masks and some even dressed as if they were going into a thick, dangerous jungle, with their socks pulled up over their pants. Their anxiety was palpable and obvious amidst their very hurried movements. Sometimes, the negative energies they emitted stuck to me and lingered in my auric field after I walked out. This is the downside of being a highly sensitive empath.

On days when I spent a couple of hours in civilization, I could feel the funk of the human world weighing on me and dragging me down. If I didn't leave as soon as I felt it happening, I would begin to feel exhausted and cranky, and like my vitality was waning. The cure was to go back to nature. I could go for a seaside stroll and let the ocean air cleanse me, or I could lay on the beach in a place where I sensed especially loving and magical energy – the sort of place a shaman might call a "power spot" – for at least twenty minutes, and make sure to stay very present and not generate any mental energy with thinking, and then the negative energy would dissolve, replaced by the lightness and unconditional love radiated by nature.

On some occasions, the side effects of dealing with civilization were more serious. There were times when I emerged from shopping trips feeling barraged with intense emotions of anxiety and hopelessness that were not my own. In these moments it felt as if a dark cloud had descended upon me and disconnected me from my light, from intuition, and from the sense of joy and serenity to which I had grown accustomed. My thoughts became the sad sort that resonated with such feelings, and I began to feel lost. In these situations, nature was not enough medicine, and so I had to call upon my spiritual healer friends for help.

In these moments they told me that they could psychically perceive entities attached to me: invisible, discarnate beings who were filled with intense, negative emotions. Entities are like spiritual leeches that float around and glob onto the human energy field like invisible amoebas, clogging up our chakras and feeding off our life force.

There are many types of entities. Some are innocent ghosts, lost souls wandering around in an alternate dimension, feeling very frightened and sad, just looking for the Heavenly portal to the Other Side and mistaking a person who channels divine light, like me, for the doorway. And in this confusion they sometimes take refuge inside a human energy field and stink it up with their bad vibes – their despair, fear, or guilt over the way they lived their life that has kept them from feeling brave enough to cross over. They also feed on your life force energy and deplete you. When this happened to me, I would notice a distinct feeling that something was very "off" inside myself, and a feeling of being very tired. Eventually I got the hang of recognizing when a ghost was in my field, and I learned to say, "You can't stay here. My light is not the portal you're looking for. The angels will help you find it," and then I'd feel a shift – a tickly tingle that started in the top of my head and zapped down through my spine – and I'd feel like myself again.

But I discovered that there are other sorts of entities that are more difficult to get rid of because they are intentionally malicious and crafty about how they haunt you. These discarnate creatures, typically not human in origin, feed off of the negative emotions we emit and therefore intentionally try to make us miserable. They may do this by planting a negative thought or radiating a lower emotion within us that we mistake for our own and then get caught up in, like depression or anxiety. (To them, fear tastes delicious.) Or they may try to dredge up our deep-seated insecurities and trigger latent psychological issues because if they can get us to regret our past or judge ourselves harshly, for instance, then they really feast, because guilt and shame are the favorite dishes of these types of creatures. (On the upside, they certainly provide helpful motivation for working out our issues as fast as we can!)

I discovered that the main tip-off that one of these buggers had attached itself to my aura was a sudden, dramatic and unprovoked shift in my psyche, like going from happy to suicidal in sixty seconds. It was much like J.K. Rowling's depiction of "dementors," the haunting ghouls that attack and control wizards in the *Harry Potter* books, by sucking out their will to live and draining their life force, causing them to forget their magical power. Often I could feel a sensation of physical pressure in various parts of my head when I picked something up. It could be kind of a dull ache or even a weird jagged, sharp sensation when a metaphysical flea hopped onto my scalp and was trying to burrow.[9]

Fortunately, I had enough detachment from my thoughts and feelings to be able to detect what was happening. Thank goodness I also always had access to the remedy: healers. I had only to contact a colleague and help would be instantly at hand. Because psychic healing technologies operate through the quantum field and are not bound by the usual limitations of time or space, my shaman friends could assist me from afar no matter where I was. Energy work is quite telepathic.

Whenever someone did a clearing for me, I would feel a tickling sensation in my head and then a dramatic and instant shift back to a healthy, balanced frame of mind and an empowered connection to my soul, as though nothing had ever gone wrong. Life was full of light again, I felt safe and secure, my mind was my own again and

---

[9]   And then much less commonly, there are also some very sophisticated, very twisted demons that engage in what could be considered psychic warfare, in that they use etheric devices to install what are essentially virus-like software programs of the psyche that create intense fear and disturbance in the recipient. The effect can look like paranoia or self-loathing in a person without any prior psychological tendencies in that direction. They do this because it is in their interest to protect their food supply, which is bad vibes and human suffering. For that reason they tend to target healers, in order to try and prevent humanity from ascending into higher frequencies. Plus, healers tend to have amplified energy fields which makes us especially bountiful sources. This type of attack actually happened to me on two occasions, and it was really terrible to endure. It felt like something was very wrong with me and I had the sort of unstable vibes going on that made strangers look sideways at me and move away in public places. It's hard to describe how awful it feels to know that something is terribly wrong with your mind and that there's some other presence in it, messing with you. My spirit guides communicated with me through dreams to alert me to what had happened. One, for instance, showed me a sneaky operative wearing a trenchcoat, like a secret agent spy, who walked by me and covertly tossed a grenade shaped like a metal rabbit into my left forearm. Metal is the element in Traditional Chinese Medicine that represents thought; rabbit is an animal symbolic in shamanism for fear. This was how I came to understand that a paranoia program had been installed, and that I needed to see a healer to remove it.

all was well. In the space of an hour, everything could shift. This was a great relief.[10]

On the other hand, I needed these sorts of clearings with ridiculous frequency, and it was very tiring to be constantly wrestling with demons and plucking them off me all the time like ticks in tall grass. This is why I decided to stop going into civilization entirely. I never got a demon infection in the wilderness. It only ever happened in towns.

I found a new park to camp in, a place where the gorgeous Siuslaw River winds through sand dunes, flower-strewn meadows and a forest of Douglas fir trees, and I chose to isolate myself there for as long as I could. I managed to remain in the wilderness in complete solitude for six weeks.

While the rest of the world was hunkering down to avoid getting infected by Covid-19 germs, I was going through a parallel lockdown of my own, isolating myself to avoid exposure to metaphysical pathogens and socially transmitted diseases of the mind.

Covid quarantine made it quite easy to get groceries delivered directly to my van, although the drivers were always a little confused when they realized my "address" led them to trailheads and parking lots at the beach. Sparrow helped me out during this time, too. She would bring me items I needed from the store and even do my laundry for me, and she'd drive it over to me washed and folded, for free. She was incredibly generous. I never really explained the details of what was going on because I thought she might think it was bananas, so I just explained that for spiritual purposes I needed to stay isolated in nature for a time, which she accepted. I missed the hot showers I used to take at her place but it was now summer, and I could go for dips in the river. The wild water was wonderfully rejuvenating.

---

[10]   (And, it left me wondering how many people might be locked up in mental hospitals, or heavily medicated on pharmaceutical drugs, who might be perfectly well if only they could see a good shaman.)

When the rhododendrons bloomed, glorious pink petals showered the forest floor and floated in the air. I felt I was truly living in paradise, and in such an environment I found it was possible to stay in a positive and healthy mental state indefinitely, and that it was effortless to stay in the present moment so that I could soak in the beauty surrounding me. When one maintains this present and positive way of being for a full moon cycle, I soon discovered, the energy you naturally radiate in your aura begins to congeal itself into a bubble of positivity. I called this my "Heaven Bubble," because that is what it feels like. When you are inside of a Heaven Bubble, you are in a blissful state of harmony with life. You are in full alignment with your soul, your Higher Self, and you radiate peace and happiness. It feels as if you are being bathed in divine love, because you are. It is a wonderful state of being.

As I began approaching the Heaven Bubble frequencies, I noticed certain songs on the radio began to play very often, specifically, Belinda Carlisle's "Heaven is a Place on Earth," and "Knockin' on Heaven's Door" by Bob Dylan. Even when I was camping in a remote spot without cell phone reception and in which even radio signals do not come through, Sparrow surprised me on the eve of a new moon with a spontaneous visit, brought her guitar, and serenaded me with that Dylan song!

After six weeks by myself, I felt firmly enough inside my Heaven Bubble to venture out into civilization again. I had the theory that it would probably act as a protective shield of positive energy around me. When I tested this idea with field trips, I found that it worked, and I also experienced the best possible reality: the store had my favorite foods on sale, I hit all the green lights, and Sparrow was in a great mood when I dropped by. But I could only stay in civilization briefly. After a couple of hours, the lower frequencies there began to take a toll and I felt I was wilting like a flower without water and I had to go back to the wilderness right away. Thus, even with a Heaven Bubble, I realized I could only handle civilization infrequently, and only for short stretches.

When I asked my spirit guides if there was anything else I could do to protect myself, they told me, "The only protection ever needed is unconditional love."

When we are mentally and emotionally in alignment with unconditional love, we exist in a realm of energy that resonates at a higher frequency than the one in which negative entities can live. It's much like how certain bacteria can only exist in an acidic body; love has a different pH level.

Negative entities can only exist where there is negative energy. They can't resonate where love is all there is.

Unconditional love is the state of being in real harmony – complete positive resonance – with oneself, other people, and the world, as well as every situation within it, past, present, and future.

This is only possible through a practice of non-judgement. Jesus said, "Judge not, lest ye yourself be judged." This is because, at the fundamental nature of reality, we are one with all that is. All beings are interconnected. Thus, when we judge anyone or anything that exists, we innately also judge ourselves. And because all that exists is an emanation of Source, if we judge the creation, then we also judge the Creator. And the Creator vibrates at the frequency of unconditional love. This is why judgment inherently creates separation from unconditional love.

The state of nonjudgmental, unconditionally loving awareness is called "Christ consciousness," and maintaining it takes great vigilance, especially at first. It is not easy. And even when we think we are seemingly succeeding at staying in positive energy mentally, praising all that is, and finding the silver lining in everything, it is still quite possible to subconsciously be harboring negativity – from unresolved baggage, resentments towards others or even oneself, or towards the state of the world and its many injustices.

Additionally, one has to make peace with the emotions that are hard to like, such as anger, guilt and shame. To deny, avoid or suppress such feelings when they arise creates separation from love; instead, those feelings have to be accepted and embraced. This was a major snag for me. I used to get frustrated if I felt them, and fear that they were lowering my consciousness.

Anger was difficult to love, for example, because I had grown up associating it with mean words and violence. One day when I was feeling angry, which I felt badly about, I walked along the ocean and noticed that the sea was radiating love regardless, just because that's Her nature. She wasn't going to stop radiating love just because I was in a mood. The ocean sends out love no matter what because unconditional love is her vibrational state. We are as free to receive Her love in anger as we are in joy. This is how I learned to see that if Mother Earth had no problem sending love to my anger, I could, too. Eventually I began to see that anger truly is a loveable emotion. Healthy anger tells us when something needs to change. It gives us the strength to assert our boundaries and the passion to rise against injustice.

Shame was even trickier to love. Shame made me feel small and bad and weak and embarrassed. Shame blocked me from feeling worthy of accepting help, grace, and answered prayers. Shame is the favorite food of hungry demons. Shame is a trap. How could I love shame?

It took a long time, but one day I realized that shame is the friend who knocks on my door to alert me when I've judged myself, and that's a blessing, because you can't judge yourself and love yourself at the same time – at least, not unconditionally.

I think the hardest emotion for me to navigate was a mix of guilt and regret that took the form of thoughts like: maybe-I'm-not-enough, maybe I'm not-living-up-to-my-potential, maybe-I-messed-up-important-opportunities-in-the-past. This uncomfortable sinking feeling in my gut visited me often during that period of my life, and I kept getting stuck in it. It was the trickiest trap to pull myself out of, especially when there were entities perpetuating these unhealthy thought loops.

So, I sought the counsel of the Tobacco spirit, because he is considered to be, in the realm of plant spirit medicine, a master teacher, one of the very wisest sages.

I opened a container of hapé, tapping a pea-sized amount of the fine-ground, gray tobacco ash powder into my palm.

I scooped it up with my V-shaped bamboo pipe, called a *kuripe (koo-ree-pay)*, pushing the powder into the open end in the direction of my heart, where I held it long enough to send up the vibration of love, respect, and thanks before pinching my right nostril shut, exhaling the air from my lungs, taking a deep breath, and then blowing into the mouthpiece of the *kuripe* and sending the snuff up into my left nostril. I repeated the process for the right.

I felt a sharp, burning sensation in my sinuses that radiated into my brain. It was similar to the sensation I felt as a child when accidentally inhaling chlorinated pool water up my nose. That harsh, caustic feeling passed, and then a sweet surge of energy swirled around my head and down my spine, and then a force like gravity pulled it down into the ground, as if a leaden anchor had dropped from my body into the core of the Earth. My heart felt open, still and centered. I felt a pathway opening up in the back of my skull, and I recognized it as a space for dialogue with a higher being.

A wise and gentle voice spoke. I heard it within myself, but it was not my voice. It was the voice of a dignified, masculine elder: Grandfather Tobacco.

The voice said: "*Who* is not enough, child?

Are the stars not enough? You are made of stars.

Is the water not enough? You are made of water.

Is the Earth not enough? You are made of Earth."

There is no self. How easy it is to forget.

27

MANIFESTING THE VAN

I had to pay for my minivan rental every night by 8 PM, which I did via a phone app. Its owner was not a company but a private party, a woman who lived in Portland and was renting out her family's extra vehicle by the day. If ever I did not have the funds to renew it, I would automatically lose my shelter. And, because of the rules of the app, my little home-on-wheels could also be booked by another person for a future date at any time. In either scenario, I would be required to drop everything and embark on a three-hour drive to return the minivan back to that overwhelming city I was so glad to have left behind me, where I would then be stuck until I could rent some other vehicle, the vast majority of which cost double what this one did. It would be a logistical boondoggle, but also upsetting because the minivan had come to feel like home, to offer some stability after a year of bouncing from place to place. So to avoid that very stressful possibility, I paid for as many nights in a row at a time as I could. This was onerous. It cost me more than nine hundred dollars a month to live in that minivan, nearly the same as rent for a studio apartment in some towns, and I didn't even own it. This was not a sustainable arrangement. I wanted a van that I could own outright, a home that couldn't be taken from underneath me at a moment's notice.

I longed for something like Sparrow's, which was a spacious Chevy G20 series model from the Nineties. How could I find one? And if I found one, how could I buy it? My income did not leave me anything left over after I paid for my nightly rental fee and food, so there was that obstacle. I had no savings, and getting a credit line was out of the question. This was a pickle, indeed, and I felt stuck.

One night when I was sleeping in a tent over at Sparrow's backyard, I swallowed capsules of my relaxation herbs, mainly passionflower and lemon balm, and I put on some binaural beats as I dozed off. I dreamed about finding a profound message in a slice of pepperoni cheese pizza, in the same way that people in Mexico sometimes see Mother Mary in toast. The message written in the pizza was, "You cannot be a victim and a creator at the same time." Talk about deep dish! My spirit guides were using humor to remind me that I needed to be mindful of the narrative I was telling myself about my circumstances. If I was going to view myself as a victim, then I would be forgetting that I had the power to change things.

Fortunately, my spirit guides were quick to help me remember how to do that. On an evening when money stress was making it difficult to fall asleep, I took kava kava capsules to calm myself and listened to some guided meditations, my usual routine, except I upped the dose to compensate for the extra anxiety I was feeling on that particular evening. Kava kava, a sedative with a long history of use by Polynesian cultures, put me into a very relaxed trance. I was gently awakened a few hours later, around 3 AM, to find that there was a divine masculine presence hovering around my consciousness. I recognized this energy as belonging to one of my invisible teachers, a Native American spirit guide. He was tuning my mind like a radio dial deep into the present moment, and then nudging me to vividly imagine buying a bottle of some expensive CBD oil I needed. And he was guiding me to really play pretend that this scene was truly happening in exactly that moment, and to amplify the visualization with a very big feeling of gratitude in my heart. Then I fell back asleep.

The next morning, I checked my email and I found that someone had booked a counseling session with me at 3 AM, and they had sent payment in an abundant amount that was more than sufficient to buy my herbs! The divine was with me, reminding me to use my God-given tools as a conscious creator of my life to manifest whatever I needed, just as indigenous shamans of long ago used to manifest rain for their people during droughts.

Because human consciousness is innately creative, the truth is that we are always manifesting. If we are worrying and visualizing worst-case scenarios, we are creating that potential future for ourselves. The metaphysical rule known as the Law of Attraction states that the external experiences we have are a magnetic reflection of our internal energetic frequencies, thoughts and emotions. Magic happens when we become aware of the vibration of our thoughts and feelings and use them intentionally with a concentrated focus towards our desired ends.

The recipe for conscious creation is simple: Ask, Believe, Receive. The asking part can be a vivid visualization like I did that night with the kava kava, using the imagination, or it can be as simple as a humble and sincere verbal prayer to Heaven requesting what is needed. It can also be done through writing. Being a writer, that is my preferred approach. Each moon begins a new cycle of energy, and so it was on a new moon that I wrote down in a notebook, "Manifesting: I am so grateful that I have a wonderful van that I own and love; it's perfect for me to live in. Thank you, Universe." I wrote these words in the present tense on purpose. In the realm of conscious creation – which some people call "quantum reality," and others call "5D," meaning the fifth dimension – time is an illusion. The past and present exist simultaneously and every moment is happening right now.

Next, I focused on the second ingredient in the recipe for manifestation: belief. I welled up a deep feeling of gratitude, an advance offering of faith that my request would be granted. I knew that sending "thank you" vibes to the Universe was a potent act of creation, in giving genuine appreciation for something that I chose to believe was really happening, a done deal already underway. It was not hard to believe that life would support me in this way. It even seemed like a natural evolution: homeless, borrowing a sedan, then renting a minivan, then owning my own. There was a kind of poetry in that, a story that made sense. After all, I thought, the model of the minivan I was living in was called an Odyssey – and what else was this journey but exactly that?

I told Sparrow that I was on the lookout for a van of my own, something just like hers, and she said she would keep an eye out for any good candidates. Some weeks later, while driving around her neighborhood, she snapped a photo of an attractive, charcoal-colored Chevy van with maroon stripes that had a for-sale sign on it and texted it to me. It was a 1992 model with a custom purple interior, including lavender carpet and curtains! I was delighted, because purple is my most favorite color, and the van was exactly like hers, just as I had wanted, except even better suited to my taste! The only snag was that it cost four thousand dollars, which I didn't have – yet.

Once again, on the next new moon, I wrote, "Thank you Universe for sending me the funds I need effortlessly and making sure that the van waits for me until I have them." This was really going to take a miracle, because not only did I not have four thousand dollars, I had filed bankruptcy a year prior and could not get a loan. So I knew that in order to make this happen, I had to really have relentlessly optimistic faith and believe that it was going to work out, somehow.

From the perspective of the quantum field, there are multiple potential parallel realities that simultaneously exist, and the one we experience is the one we resonate with through our beliefs and emotions. So instead of indulging negativity and worry, or allowing myself to fret about not having any idea how money could come, I did the opposite: I visualized myself having the money and focused on really embodying the feeling of having it *now* as often as I could. I thought, "What would it feel like to have four thousand dollars?"

And the answer I came up with was that I would feel relieved, happy and with a sense of spaciousness in my life.

I knew that I could reverse-engineer the prosperity I wanted by feeling as though I already had it. So, I focused on cultivating these feelings of relaxation, happiness, and spaciousness in my life in the present moment. I watched funny, uplifting movies on the little DVD player in the minivan. I read the *Harry Potter* books and *The Lion, The Witch, and the Wardrobe* series. I listened to music while drawing dragonflies and fuschia flowers. I did this not just because it was fun but also because I knew that making art strengthens the right brain, the part of our neurology that is positive and creative, and that these mental muscles can counteract tendencies towards worry. I also took my calming herbs regularly, when it did arise.

My approach worked quite effectively. Before the full moon, I read a news story that informed me of funding for self-employed people like myself. I applied for it and it turned out that I qualified for exactly four-thousand dollars, which was the precise amount I needed. I was then able to buy the van! And just as I had written, it all came with ease. In the space of a couple months, I now had my own vehicle and my own home. No matter that they were one and the same, I felt downright prosperous. (And, I didn't have to go back to Portland to return my rental. Sparrow did it for me as a paid gig. She had wanted to go there anyhow, so it was a win-win.)

Sparrow and I had a little housewarming party together in my new van on the beach. She burned a sage bundle to cleanse the old vibes in there, and then she bedazzled it for me by gluing a little Buddha figurine on the dashboard, along with amethyst, fluorite and rose quartz crystals. The interior was taller and broader than the minivan I had been renting. In the minivan I could only crawl around and it was fairly narrow in width. There was very little space, but this new vehicle was so spacious I could actually sprawl out and do full yoga poses in it! Between that and the curtains and the carpet, it really felt like a proper home! I was so delighted. Finally, I had stability again.

28

PARASITES

If you are at all outdoorsy then you probably already know that it isn't safe to drink wild water from a stream unless you boil it first. But when Sparrow told me I could drink the water where I was camping, I mistakenly thought she meant it was OK to consume raw. I drank quite a lot of it, and subsequently got very sick with chills, a fever, major intestinal distress, and dysentery.

First I turned to herbs for help. I swallowed capsules of oregano oil and Oregon grape root that I had on hand, because I knew these were antimicrobial herbs that can be used to kill bacteria in the gut. These medicines got rid of the fever and chills within a couple days, but the dysentery continued. It persisted for weeks, with an unusual odor that indicated an infection. There was also a worrisome stinging and stabbing sensation in my intestines. A phrase came to me intuitively: "ulcerative colitis." Sometimes I get these clairaudient phrases and then I look them up and I discover what they mean. And in this case it certainly fit. Ulcerative colitis means inflammation of the colon, with ulcers. As I researched further I discovered that if left untreated, waterborne parasites could indeed cause ulcerative colitis.

I thought perhaps I should go to a doctor and get antibiotics, because the herbs did not appear to be killing whatever was making me ill. I went to an urgent care clinic. The doctor was surprisingly dismissive. He didn't believe me when I said I had gotten sick drinking from wild water. He said that I was probably imagining things and had just eaten something that upset my stomach. He didn't want to run a diagnostic test or discuss medication. He treated me like he was the expert on my body because he had a medical degree, and because I didn't, I was necessarily ill-informed.

This disappointing, disempowering experience left me feeling frustrated at how readily the mainstream medical system devalues a patient's connection to her own body and her intuition about what is happening within it. I have heard many similar stories from other people who have experienced this same sort of arrogance from conventional doctors, sometimes to life-threatening detriment. I wasn't going to let that happen to me.

Something was wrong. I had dysentery and sharp pains in my bowels, and it wasn't the kind of thing that happened to me from food sensitivities. I went for a walk in nature and asked the Universe to show me what to do. I saw two big dead frogs on my hike, and I took them as an answer.

I gave myself two kambo treatments. After the first treatment, my intestines stopped hurting. After the second, my digestion returned to normal. Of course kambo would work, with its potent germ-killing effects and its ability to promote healing. I asked myself why I had not thought to use it sooner. I suppose it was because I had been chastened by my experiences of overuse, and did not want to risk getting insomnia again unless I felt sure it was an appropriate remedy, divinely guided.

I was so happy to have my health back, and I thought, "It's no wonder eighty percent of the world relies upon natural medicine.[11] Natural medicine works."

---

[11]   That statistic comes from a 2014 article in the academic journal *Frontiers in Pharmacology* by Martins Ekor.

29

MIRACLES IN YACHATS

The stretch of coastal highway north of Florence is filled with rocky beaches and little clusters of Douglas fir forests abutting them in which one can camp for free, as I did. When you drive further north, you pass a place where the sea whips and swirls against the rocky cliffs called Thor's Well, and then eventually you reach the tiny town of Yachats, Oregon, a tourist enclave thick with sea fog and rainbows. A rock with a big sign on it as you approach Yachats informs you that this little village is "The Gem of the Oregon Coast."

In October the rainy season begins and so, feeling rather weary of van camping in damp conditions, I was eager for the comfort of a hot bath and a kitchen, and I decided to treat myself to a few nights at a motel. I stopped into the first one I passed by, a place called the Yachats Inn. At the front desk, the clerk handed me a key and said, "You will be staying in the Lily Pad building, in the Green Frog Suite." The frog suite? Really?

When I opened the door to the suite and turned on the TV, a cartoon movie called *The Princess and the Frog* was playing.

The next day, I got a phone call from an acquaintance in Portland who knew I was living at the coast, asking if I would facilitate a frog medicine retreat here for a group of her friends who liked to drink ayahuasca together, as soon as possible.

I said yes, of course, and I wondered where exactly to give them kambo. Maybe on the beach? As I walked the grounds of the inn, I discovered that it had a very lovely event space with views of the crashing waves that would be perfect for the kambo ceremony. I booked it, and everything lined up so that they were able to come there the next weekend.

As I sat next to a little pond at the Inn and marveled at this magical turn of events, a gray-haired woman staying in the suite next door to my own came outside and struck up a casual conversation with me. She told me she had just arrived at the ocean from Portland, where she had visited a metaphysical store called New Renaissance – the very one I used to teach at and do intuitive readings at. She said she had just purchased a painting of Green Tara that she wanted to show me.

30

PALM DESERT

I knew it was time to leave Oregon when autumn thunderstorms struck the coast, pounding down rain and rocking my van with strong winds. I had been living beside the ocean for nine months, and now that it was the rainy season, I was ready to go and begin my journey to the dry, sunny Southwest. My plan was to drive south along the 101 coastal highway through California until the beauty of a place touched my heart and inspired me to stay.

The first place this happened was among the rolling hills of Carmel Valley, a gorgeous swath of wine country in central California. The dry climate of this region was refreshing after steeping in the heavy dampness of the Northwest for so long. I stopped to hike at Garland Ranch, a regional park filled with acres of stately sycamore and oak trees that radiated tranquility, which was exactly what I was looking for. But Carmel Valley did not easily lend itself to van life. I stealth-camped along highway sides mostly, spending my days hiking the many scenic trails there and wandering around Carmel Valley Village, a small rural town about thirteen miles inland from the ocean. I was particularly fond of the Little Free Library boxes I found there, which furnished me with some excellent reading material.

I love those colorful cabinets because they contain a delightfully unpredictable, eclectic assortment within them. When I find one of these boxes, I scan the shelves inside for a title that stands out to me. Sometimes the words will catch me and other times a book just seems to have a glow about it. The book nook in that little town was especially bountiful for me. I found many good reads, including *Angels in My Hair,* a captivating memoir by a clairvoyant Irish woman who talks about having vivid conversations with these great winged beings. The author, Lorna Byrne, writes that God is always sending angels down to Earth to answer our prayers and make life better for us, but that there are many "unemployed" angels here because Earth is a free-will zone, and Heaven is not allowed to intervene in our lives without our express permission. After I read that, I began to speak to them each morning to grant my permission for divine intervention every day and as I did so, a shower of grace did come upon me. Strangers knocked on my door and offered food, friendship, and to give out their phone numbers just in case I ever needed a shower or felt unsafe.

In this town I was certainly the only person living in a van that I saw, and I camped in parking lots and on highway sides and on the fringes of residential neighborhoods, which made for a very awkward feeling given that I was surrounded by million-dollar houses and other trappings of luxury. The prices at the local grocery store were many times what I was used to seeing. I felt less like a fortunate free spirit living in the paradise of nature, and more like someone who was down-and-out, and kind of squatting. Living like that in opulent California was difficult. I had to be careful of the way I saw my circumstances because it was easy to feel down and out instead of free and blessed, especially on cold mornings when I woke up freezing cold, out of propane for heat and breathing vapor clouds in the air. Poverty and simplicity are next-door neighbors, and sometimes the line that divides them is hard to see. Self-compassion is a bulwark in such times, but self-pity is a path that leads only to despair. Perception is everything.

Another book I read in Carmel Valley was *The Help* by Kathryn Stockett, which aside from being a great novel, describes a character who writes her prayers instead of speaking them, like me, and who is very good at getting her prayers answered. The character uses her ability to help others, as an act of service. She helps people with their health and other life situations. I felt that my spirit guides were nudging me and reminding me to do the same, so I began to do that more often, to intentionally manifest good things not just for myself, but for others who are struggling with similar situations, and also the world as a whole. It made sense. "Thank you, Universe, for making Earth a place where we learn and grow through joy instead of pain and suffering," I wrote. "Thank you for blessing humanity with the technology to live in harmony with the Earth, and the political climate to implement it. Thank you for bringing peace where there is war. Thank you for ending poverty."

After several weeks I drove south again, stopping to go hiking in Palm Desert, a place that looks exactly the way it sounds: sand-colored hills dotted with palm trees, and cute little road runner birds all over the place. (They are normal bird size, not giant like in the cartoons). When I arrived at a trailhead there I was surprised to find that it had the unusual feature of sharing a parking lot with a Baptist church. I slept there, and the next day, someone knocked on my door. "I'm the pastor of this church," the man said. "I just wanted to tell you that you're welcome to stay here, and we'd love it if you'd like to come to our Christmas Eve service. You can bring your dog, too."

I knew it was December but living as I was, I hadn't realized that it was Christmas Eve! His invitation was quite welcome. Though I was not raised in Christianity, I have deep respect and appreciation for Jesus, a great teacher who modeled forgiveness, mercy and unconditional love. I have enjoyed meditating with his presence and called upon him during healing sessions, so I was more than happy to celebrate his life with his followers. Human contact was appealing, too, and this particular church was anti-mask, so I got to actually see people's faces, which was refreshing. Now that I wasn't living in the wilderness and didn't have those cheerful ocean vibes to uplift me, I had actually felt lonely.

Sometimes, when I was feeling down, my mind would ruminate about the past, reviewing choices I could have made differently and feeling regret, and concentrating on painful times I felt unhappy about. I knew this was not good for my mental health, and I tried to rally out of it, and I used my herbs, but it was still a struggle, and I felt overwhelmed by it. Whether this gloomy period was caused by entity infections or it was just my own unresolved baggage coming to the surface, I couldn't be sure, but even if it was the former, it was only possible because the latter existed.

As it happened, the pastor's sermon that night contained a message that I really needed to hear. He said that being human means being imperfect, and God understands that and loves us anyway. He extends mercy to us even when we feel undeserving of it because that is His nature. From the divine perspective, we are loved simply because we are His children, his creations, and all that is asked in return is our gratitude.

As I lay down to sleep at night, I felt a loving presence come upon me. As I relaxed into a meditative state, I felt invisible beings with good vibes moving around my head, tinkering. I felt them wipe clean the neurological grooves and circuits in my brain that had been worn deep with old patterns of self-judgment, self-criticism and regret, forged in unhealthy ways of thinking that, try as I did, I had not been able to stop. When I awoke the next morning, I felt psychologically upgraded, gentler to myself. I was well again, in a way I hadn't been in a long time.

I slept in that church parking lot in Palm Desert for another week or so, hiking the desert trails with Daisy, until the pastor told me the neighbors living in the mansions nearby were complaining about the van in the parking lot. They didn't like the appearance of a "transient person." After a Sunday service he handed me a hundred dollars and bid me farewell on my travels, and that is when I set off for Arizona.

31

JACKPOT

A rizona is filled with public wild land that allows free camping, and as you drive the highways that span its sprawling desertscapes, you see an abundance of trailers and vans dotting the sand-and-gravel hills that line them. The people inside them are "boondocking," also called "dry camping," which means living off-the-grid and soaking up power from the sun through solar panels on their rooftops, or living without electricity entirely.

I first saw this while driving southwards from Lake Havasu. When I stopped to buy some water in the scrub desert town of Parker, Arizona, a little place I thought I was just passing through, my engine died. I tried to turn the key in the ignition but all that did was make sad noises. A few kind passersby heard the sounds of my struggling motor and came over to help out. After tinkering under the hood, these folks advised me that the trouble was most likely a broken flywheel, which is apparently a big deal. When I called the local shops, I discovered that this was going to be an expensive repair: they estimated ten hours of labor, plus parts. And I would have to wait. They were all booked a month out!

I sensed that this turn of events wasn't an accident. I had parked directly right in front of the Colorado River Indian Tribes museum, because it was in the same strip mall as the Safeway grocery store and a CVS convenience store. Technically Parker is sandwiched within an "Indian" reservation, land shared by the Hopi, Navajo, Chemehuevi and Mojave nations. In a sense, it kind of seemed like I had just been stopped in my tracks by the ancestors of this land. I thought of a bumper sticker I'd seen once that said, "Oh no! Not another learning experience!"

I was stranded at the strip mall parking lot for several days. At least I could use the bathroom facilities at the supermarket and the drugstore. In the drugstore, I saw a poster that said, "Attitude is everything. Choose a good one," and I began to feel pretty sure that this was another one of those initiations Spirit had decided I needed to go through.

I went in and out of that Safeway grocery store a lot and so I began to get to know the staff. When I explained that I was living in the parking lot because my van had broken down, they suggested I have it towed to the nearby Bluewater Casino, which was just over a mile away and allowed visitors to camp for free in motorhomes, trailers and vans in the parking lot.

The Bluewater Casino turned out to be a blessing for me. It sits directly on the eastern bank of the Colorado River, which makes it quite pretty and scenic, actually. The grounds are dotted with palm trees and there are red agates and quartz crystals glittering in the ground. The place has a festive feeling to it, too, because it's a casino, so it has that upbeat party vibe going for it. All things considered, it added up to being a pretty great place to be stuck, if I had to be stuck.

The first gift the casino brought me was community. I had been on my own until this time, usually with no other van-lifers in sight. The casino was filled with other people living in their cars, vans and motorhomes full-time, too, just like me. It was like a little village. As I walked around and got to know everybody, I found that most of my neighbors were retired, living on fixed incomes, and staying here because they were thrifty "snowbirds" living in the sunshine over the winter. A few were younger people working remotely over their laptops, or trading in the stock market. Some were just barely getting by on disability payments from the government. They spanned all corners of the political and religious spectrum, though they tended to consistently become independent do-it-yourself types, and the prepper element was well-represented. A few people I met had given up big houses and fancy possessions to be traveling, van-dwelling minimalists. They had been inspired, they told me, by a man named Bob Wells, an influencer who has a wildly popular YouTube channel called "Cheap RV Living," and who founded an annual community meetup called the Rubber Tramp Rendezvous in Quartzsite, Arizona. The unconventional nature of this lifestyle was a shared point of pride, and I learned that there was a name for us: "Nomads."

The nomads I met there were in general very friendly and helpful. When people found out my van was broken down, they did things to try and help me, like drop off drinking water. As I got to know the village customs a little bit better, I learned that most people were introverts like myself who needed a lot of alone time, and that the unspoken etiquette was that it is most respectful to approach people only when they are outside and signaling receptivity to social interaction, rather than by knocking or approaching them when they are inside their vans and motorhomes. I liked that custom and I fit right in.

The highlight of each day was always the spectacular rainbow-colored sunsets. (It was actually Daisy who got me noticing them. She always made a point to sit and watch them.)

Soon sunset-watching became a nightly ritual I did not just with Daisy, but also my new friend Karen, a retired nurse. She is a unique juxtaposition of both right-wing, fundamentalist Christian and easygoing, open-minded pothead with quick wit, an arsenal of jokes always at the ready. For instance, one day I wasn't feeling so well because there was a traffic jam in my bowels, and Karen quipped: "Shit happens. Eventually."

Karen liked to surprise me with gifts of food for myself and my dog Daisy on mornings when I was writing. When I asked her why she did that, especially given that she was living on a fixed income, Karen said, "If you read the Bible, God says we're supposed to help each other." When she left town one day, as I learned that nomad friends inevitably do, I felt quite sad. Karen was the first friend I'd met in six months.

It was a very hot day, so I decided to go for a walk into town and duck inside an air conditioned big-box store. I paused at a display of hair-straightening irons, and I struck up a conversation with a friendly-looking woman shopping next to me. "Do you know if these are any good?" I asked her.

"I don't, but I have some very expensive straightening irons I don't use at home. I can go and get them for you," she said.

"Really?" I asked. This was quite a generous offer.

"Sure, or you can come over to my house if you'd like," she said.

"OK, why not? That sounds like fun," I said.

I wouldn't normally hop into a stranger's pickup truck and trot off to their house without at least knowing them first, but I accepted her offer because I could read her energy intuitively and it was easy to see that she had a genuinely good-hearted nature with no motivation beyond kindness. This turned out to be a very good decision. On the drive, my new friend stopped at a grocery store and bought fresh salmon to cook for my dog, and then she handed me a hundred-dollar bill! When we got to her house, she showed me the array of high-end luxury cars in her garage and introduced me to her many rescued housecats. Then she showered me with gifts: designer perfume, a gorgeous leopard print handbag, a pair of matching high heels, and lovely turquoise jewelry. She seemed to delight in giving her things away, and was even a little giddy about it.

"I have to pay it forward because I am very blessed," she said. "I win at the casino all the time. Just this year I won $5,000, $20,000, and $10,000 on nickel slots!"

"Really?" I asked. "What's your secret?"

"At first I wondered if I was about to die or something because it was so eerie," she said. "But then I talked with other people who win a lot and they all say you have to go in there without hoping to win and have fun just playing, and that's what I do."

Ah, she is very good at practicing non-attachment, I thought.

Meeting this woman was very inspiring. While I didn't feel in my heart that gambling was my particular path to divinely guided prosperity, I did try playing a few slot machines after I met her to see if maybe something might happen. It didn't, of course. It wasn't much fun for me; I just ended up donating spare change to the tribes that owned the games. But I did sense that the energy of the Bluewater Casino would be auspicious for me, and I knew just how I could harness its aura of good tidings.

Most of my neighbors lived in spacious motorhomes that they could walk around in. They slept on actual beds inside them, real mattresses, and they could cook on a stove, refrigerate their food, sit at a proper table to eat their meals, and even use a toilet and a shower. They had running water and lights inside, electricity powered by the sun. My broken down van was seeming so shoddy in comparison, a small metal hut that offered shelter but no amenities. I wanted to improve my living situation very badly, as soon as possible. I wanted to be able to stand up inside and bathe some place other than a truck stop. I was ready to go from camping to glamping.

I pondered the logistics of how I could pull this off. My money situation was still very tight, so it seemed I'd have to sell my van in order to get funds and then look for a motorhome. But where would I live without my van? I could stay in the casino hotel, but that was not very appealing to me because it would disconnect me from the living-in-nature vibes I thrive in and expose me to an overload of electromagnetic frequencies and indoor life. Even if I accepted the stress and disruption in my routine short-term, how long might the process take? What if it took a while and ate up my funds for the motorhome? And how would I even get to look at a potential motorhome if I had already sold my van? The more I thought about it, the more overwhelming these many variables seemed to become.

Then I had an epiphany: I could swap my van directly for a proper motorhome, without any money involved. That way, I would never be without a home again. And how would I make sure I got an RV that was perfectly suited to my needs and tastes, at an exactly equivalent price point? I could manifest it, of course. It would seem to take a miracle to make everything work out, but miracles are not so hard to come by when you're willing to believe in them. My magic is the magic of words, so I wrote in my journal, "Creating: Thank you Universe, for sending me an RV that I absolutely love, that's perfect for me in every way. I'm so grateful that it came to me for free!"

Then I posted an ad listing my van for sale on social media, and I wrote that it was worth four thousand dollars but that I wanted to trade it for a motorhome instead of receiving a cash payment. Someone out there had to want the same thing, in reverse. Maybe they had a house and they didn't need a motorhome. Maybe they wanted to downsize.

My next step was to have relentless faith, so I gave thanks every day and did all I could to convince my imagination that the swap was already underway imminently. There were moments when doubts did creep in, and I felt bursts of despair when I imagined how depressing it would be to stay stuck living in a broken down van in a parking lot, especially when the weather began heating up in the spring. I did my best not to entertain these negative imaginings because I knew they would only bring me down and block the bandwidth for miracles to flow by aligning me with a reality that I did not want to create. Instead, I gave myself compassion when fears and doubts did arise, without buying into them, and then visualized how good it would feel when I finally had my new RV. In other words, I tried to reverse-worry.

At the same time, I also had to be careful not to let myself get frustrated with my current situation. I had to love what I had, while looking forward to what would come next, because if I resented my van, I would be in resistance to the flow. Negative energy blocks the bandwidth for miracles. Longing, too, emanates the vibration of lack, and that frequency is a trap that manifests not-having. So when my mind got stuck in wanting, I knew I needed to shift my focus, so in those moments I went to visit with friends, watched TV shows on my cell phone, listened to podcasts and read books. If I still couldn't, sometimes I asked Jeanette, my old Reiki mentor, to send positive vibes my way, and that always helped, too.

After a couple weeks, a young, pregnant woman from San Diego named Erica reached out to me offering to swap my van for her vintage motorhome. She said she had purchased it used earlier in the year but that she didn't use it much and didn't like driving such a large, gas-guzzling vehicle when she did, so the idea of trading it for a cute little van sounded great to her. Erica sent me a photo of a 21-foot Class C motorhome – that's the kind that has a bed over the "cab," the front driver and passenger seats – and it had the works: a bathroom, shower, fridge, oven, stove, a table with booth seats, and multiple beds in it. It was made of fiberglass instead of metal, which meant it wouldn't heat up the way most vehicles do in the sun. It had big windows running the length of the walls, so I could still feel very connected to nature, and not like I was separate from it, trapped indoors. It was a unique, obscure model from 1982 that had a kind of retro charm to it.

I thought: Jackpot!

However, there was the issue of how I could find a way to get my broken down van road-worthy for Erica. Because once again, I had very little money. A stroke of luck came through my parents. Though we had been estranged, they spontaneously reached out to me in a loving and generous mood and asked if there was anything they could do to help me. Dad was feeling apologetic about how harsh he had been in my childhood and wanted to make amends. I told them my situation, and they happily gifted me the money for the repairs I needed. By another miracle, I was actually able to get an appointment with a local mechanic to fix it.

A third miracle came when Erica, the woman with the RV, agreed to drive it five hours from San Diego to meet me in Parker! This meant I didn't have to worry about finding gas money to get to California. She arrived at night on the eve of a new moon and we met under the stars in the desert. We wrote out handwritten receipts stating that we were gifting our vehicles to each other. It felt like a meeting blessed by divine grace, and I believe it was.

32

ROGER & LYN

At first, I was very glad about the swap. Erica, the woman who traded my van for her RV, had assured me that my new motorhome was in "great shape mechanically" but that it had not been used much recently and would need "a lot of love." I hadn't understood exactly what she meant by that – perhaps that it needed to be imbued with positive energy? Her euphemism became more clear when I turned the key in the ignition and exhaust fumes spewed into the cabin. Apparently "love" meant repairs. When I asked mechanically inclined neighbor friends to take a look under the hood for me, they said rather than being in "great shape mechanically," my new home was actually in terrible shape mechanically and barely drivable at all – dangerous, even. Some people even said it was too messed up to fix, which was just about the worst thing I could imagine. Oh, what a bummer this was!

Had I just been tricked? I prefer to think that Erica, the woman who had given me my new home, was innocent and ignorant and simply didn't know it was in such poor shape, because she had after all just driven it. But I am not sure if that's really true, because when I tried to get in touch with her, she ignored my calls and texts and effectively disappeared into thin air. Maybe she knowingly dumped a lemon on me, or maybe she hadn't but couldn't muster the courage to face it. I didn't know what to do, so I broke down and cried.

"Honey, let's pray together," my friend Lyn said on one such day. She took my hands inside hers and said, "Dear Lord, please bring the perfect people to help her with her vehicle."

Lyn was my neighbor. She lived with her husband, Roger, in the back of a rusty old pickup truck with a cracked windshield. They slept under a topper they had improvised out of pressed particle board and duct tape. We had met when I was handing out free food from the local food bank to my neighbors; they had given me way more than I needed and so I tried to help distribute the largesse. To my surprise, very few of the nomads nearby even wanted it. I guess I was one of the only people in my situation and the rest had plenty of money to buy their groceries. But Roger and Lyn were appreciative and they tipped me off to the hotspots of the local dumpster diving situation, and lucky for me, they knew where the fresh avocados were at.

Soon we were foraging together and walking across the desert to Walmart and hanging out at each other's camp spots. They were a lot of fun to talk with. Lyn struck me as very caring and heart-centered. Roger has a great sense of humor and a lot of wisdom. He tosses out the kind of gems a writer can really appreciate, like, "You don't know that God is all you need until God is all you have." I enjoyed listening to their deep Southern accents, which to me, having been raised on the East Coast and then living my adult life in Oregon, sounded charming, kind of exotic and novel. (Lyn is from Alabama and Roger's from Texas). The two of them used to be truck drivers at one point and that's how they met, at a truck stop eatery. Lyn looked to be in her late forties or early fifties, with bright blond hair and skin tanned by the sun. Roger is a decade older and usually wearing a gray, baseball-type cap. After having lived for so long in a city obsessed with being hip, I found their unpretentious nature very refreshing. They seemed like folks who had grown up in rural places and were used to roughing it, relying on their creativity and resourcefulness to get by. They did not pity themselves nor lament their circumstances in the least. Instead, they treated life like an adventure.

Roger does handyman type stuff for people they know, repairing broken things, and much of it he does for free, out of kindness, because a lot of people can't afford to pay. Lyn gets disability payments from the government. Her hobby is making jewelry. Lyn had injured feet yet she walked everywhere, as I did. She never complained about it, but the pain she was in sometimes left her relying on the kindness of strangers. Somehow, she was never short of helpers. Lyn is as steeped in grace as anyone I ever met. One day after we walked to the supermarket together, she sat down on a bench and got approached with offers for free rides instantly, within a minute. No exaggeration. She didn't even have to ask. People just saw her hobbling and wanted to help.

"Wow," I said. "God really takes care of you."

"Yes, He does," Lyn replied.

"Come talk to my friend Sedona. She's visiting later," she added.

Just before dusk I saw Lyn and Roger sitting in their camping chairs, cooking spaghetti and meatballs next to their truck. They were joined by an elderly woman who I supposed was Sedona.

"Sit right here, honey," Lyn said, patting a chair.

"Thank you, Lyn," I said, "But I'd rather sit right here on the ground."

"What are you, an Apache?" Roger quipped.

"I just like to be close to the Earth," I said. "It feels good."

"So this must be your friend Sedona?" I asked.

"Yes, I am," Sedona answered.

After we exchanged some pleasantries, the talk turned to my car troubles.

"Everything is solvable," Roger said. "God gives us problems. The problems don't stop. We solve a problem and a new one appears. God gives us these problems for a reason."

"God answers all of our prayers. Just believe, and tell Him you love Him," Sedona said.

"If He's God, why would He want us to tell Him we love Him?" I asked her.

"Because he's your father. He likes to hear that," Sedona said.

She continued, "Be very specific. I asked God to help me get my disability payments. Then I had two strokes and a heart attack! I should have said, 'Please help me get disability like I am now.'"

We laughed together. But really, Sedona said, those experiences were also blessings. For one thing she ended up in a nursing home where she had a chance to blow the whistle on a drunken, abusive orderly whom she was able to get fired, which helped the patients who were more timid. And for another thing, that heart attack gave her a round-trip ticket to Heaven.

"I died," she said. "I went to Paradise. It's not like it is here. It's very peaceful."

She came back with deep faith.

"Anything you ask God to do, He will do. All He asks is that we love Him," Sedona said. "There was a fire coming towards my house. I prayed and the wind blew it away. Then someone interrupted my prayer and it came back. So I prayed again, and it blew away again. Believe. God loves us so much. He knows we are not perfect like Jesus. Every night give thanks to Him. And try to be a little better every day, to make Him proud. And even if you fail, He is still proud," Sedona said.

"And when good things happen, say, 'God allowed this.' Don't take credit. Don't say, 'I did this,'" she added.

I was grateful to have met Sedona and I hurried back to my vehicle to write it all down in a notebook, so I wouldn't forget her words.

While I waited for our prayers to get answered, I set out to make my situation feel as positive as possible. I focused on fixing the things that were within my control and my budget. For instance, the stock upholstery that covered the ceiling and the walls was a vintage velour in unfortunate shades of brown and chartreuse. This thing was afterall born in the early Eighties, like me. So I walked a mile to the local Walmart and bought a few yards of pretty pink and purple fabrics, and some push pins, and then I walked back and got to work on giving my new nest a makeover. When I was done, I was very pleased.

Then I set my sights on addressing the exterior, which was beige with brown and orange stripes across it – the farthest thing from my aesthetic. I felt inspired by the spectacular desert sunsets I got to witness each day at dusk, so I went to Walmart again and bought spray paint in bright pink, purple, and gold. Now it was a huge art project with a unique mural all over it, and life felt like it was on the upswing again. Though I could hardly drive it, at least I could enjoy looking at it.

33

THE DOOR

My new motorhome not only had an overwhelming number of mechanical problems, it also had no door. There was a gaping hole on the side of the vehicle where an entry to the living quarters should have been, with just a bit of wire, a sheet of plastic, and a tapestry covering it. To get into the cabin, I had to climb over the front seats. Considering everything, this seemed like a relatively minor issue to me – until the early spring windstorms swept through the desert with 50 mph blasts. Then the lack of a door became a more pressing problem. I learned to determine the wind direction and then reposition my camper accordingly, so that the gusts would strike the solid side of the vehicle instead of the opening covered with thin fabric.

Some of my nomad neighbors, seeing the urgency of my situation, tried to build a door for me, but each time, it fell apart. First Roger built me a door made of thin particle board, but then someone else offered to improve upon it and in so doing, unfortunately destroyed it, because it turned out he didn't actually know what he was doing. (Roger was understandably offended, and he didn't want to build it twice). Another neighbor had a particularly creative idea. He tried installing a discarded closet door from someone's house in town, but it turned out that it was way too heavy and bulky to fit on the hinges.

When I had a little money coming in again I tried to hire a local carpenter, but the guy totally flaked out and didn't show up at all, saying he was busy and didn't feel like doing the project. Next I tried ordering an actual RV door from a used parts store on the internet, because it was an obscure model with unusual dimensions. Though it was eight hundred dollars, it seemed like the only option. Once it arrived, I hired another handyman to help me install it – only to find that it didn't fit, either!

"Really, Universe?!" I thought.

Then it dawned on me. Maybe everything was happening like this on purpose. Maybe this was one of those God-given problems Roger had talked about. Maybe it was not an accident that I was in yet another situation that required a miracle to fix. Maybe that was the point. I started to feel like I was some kind of reverse Samantha from the classic TV show "Bewitched." Whereas she was a blonde who was not allowed to use her magical gifts to solve problems, I was a brunette with the opposite situation going on. It seemed that life just wouldn't let me use worldly approaches to make things happen, and I was being forced to use divine magic, by which I mean the focused and intentional use of consciousness – with a big dollop of divine grace.

OK, I thought, I can do this. I can manifest a door. I wrote in my journal: "Thank you, Universe, for giving me a door," and then I resigned myself to waiting for divine timing, because I knew I had no other choice. I gave up trying to make anything happen, settled into some good books, and practiced faith and gratitude. I sure did wonder how and when that much-needed door would come to me.

As it happened, the divine had a very interesting plan. On a weekend afternoon, I walked my dog and noticed some new arrivals to our parking lot village. These tie-dye wearing nomad neighbors stuck out not just because of their colorful attire but for being in their forties rather than their sixties and seventies like most people I knew. When I stopped to chat with them, I learned that they had come to Parker to sell their handmade didgeridoos at the local farmers market. Given that the didgeridoo is an aboriginal musical instrument that often accompanies psychedelic type ceremonies, I wondered how much we had in common. I asked if they had ever heard of kambo before, and to my surprise, there was one person in the group who had. I'll call him Jason. Jason is a tall, broad-shouldered guy with shoulder-length blond locks who looks a little bit like Kurt Cobain. Jason said that actually he was really eager to get a frog medicine treatment and had been looking for a practitioner. His goal was to quit smoking cigarettes and he knew that kambo medicine is known for helping with that. As I got to know him better, I discovered that, amazingly, he just happened to be a professional carpenter, too!

I didn't even have to ask him for help on the door. He saw the situation and took the initiative on a day with an extremely powerful windstorm in the forecast. He went to the hardware store and custom-built a door for me out of plywood that fit the door-frame's unusual dimensions, just in the nick of time.

I facilitated some kambo ceremonies to help Jason quit smoking and we stayed in touch. He reached out to say that it had worked, he gave up cigarettes successfully and he also gave up drinking, too. He even made the brave decision to let go of his tribe of traveling friends and fly solo, because they partied a lot and he knew that wasn't the best influence for his new health goals. He had started jogging and making art again, too, and he said his biggest priority was now to develop his intuitive gifts and become the shamanic healer he knew he was meant to be. This was all wonderful news, and it was not surprising to hear, because as it detoxes your body, kambo also helps you align with your soul, which makes it easier to follow its guidance.

I was left with no question as to whether our meeting had been divinely aligned.

And so, I no longer doubted whether the boondoggle in the engine could be solved. True, seven mechanics in a row had declined to work on it, saying that it was too much trouble, but I knew I only had to use some magic and then wait patiently. So I wrote, "Thank you, Universe, for fixing my engine."

The key got stuck in the ignition one afternoon when I was driving through a country-western town a couple hours away. I tried to park but I couldn't turn the engine off, so I stopped at an auto shop there for emergency help. The mechanics not only got the ignition switch fixed, they also turned out to be willing to tackle the messed up engine, too. And it did get repaired. Now, I could drive without exhaust fumes spewing into the cabin.

I began to realize that with divine magic, maybe every problem really *does* have a solution.

34

THE BIKE

One afternoon when I was out running errands around Parker, I stopped at a gas station for fuel. I went into the little convenience store there to pay in cash, and when I came out, I noticed that my pink bicycle, which was normally mounted on the back of my vehicle, had gone missing.

"Oh, hell no," I said. "Someone did *not* just take my bike!" Anger rose up inside me, and then I had an idea.

There is a technique called "lucid dreaming" in which we can use our awareness and conscious intention to mold what happens next in our sleep time adventures. Shamans say that our waking life is a dream, too, and that the only difference is that we dream this one together with each other, co-creating consensus reality into form. If this is true, then in theory it would be possible to lucid dream while we are awake, too. We could narrate what will happen next and write the story of our lives as it is unfolding in the present moment.

I decided to try.

"I cannot be stolen from," I declared. "I now live in a parallel reality in which it's simply not possible. In fact, the police are about to find my bicycle and return it to me immediately."

I called the Parker police department and e-mailed them a photo of my distinctive bike, which I had spray painted pink with gold glitter.

It was a cross between a mountain bike and a road bike, with hand brakes and a big comfy seat.

Within an hour they called me back with excellent news: My bike had been found! The thief abandoned it on the sidewalk at a major intersection, where the cops had spotted it easily. Apparently the perpetrator had been struck with a sudden change of heart.

I was thrilled, but I wasn't too surprised that this technique had worked. I already used it all the time to solve more minor problems. When I misplace my keys, I say, "I'm so glad I'm about to find my keys." And then I do. My eye falls upon them, or an image of their whereabouts instantly pops into my mind. I just hadn't tried it on something bigger before.

I call this technique "quantum jumping," because it entails hopping between parallel realities in the multiverse that is our world. I do it through the power of words.

Storytelling is a natural human tendency, and it is one that we can harness it to our benefit. So often we limit ourselves to what is possible, caging ourselves inside ideas that feel like iron bars when in fact the rules of our reality are as changeable as thoughts themselves.

It's like a game – a game of pretend that, actually, I remember playing as a little girl. My younger sister and I would sit inside my bedroom closet, and I would announce, "When I open the door, we're going to be in a parallel universe that looks exactly the same as this one but is in fact slightly different." Even then, we were quantum jumping.

From an array of potential possibilities, we align ourselves with an outcome by witnessing it before it happens, just like the quantum physicists who discovered that energy can take the form of a particle or a wave, and that which one it becomes depends entirely on observer bias. If the scientist expected to find a wave, a wave was detected. If the scientist expected to find a particle, a particle was detected.

We are both the narrators and the protagonists of our lives. We get to give meaning and context to what we experience. And often, we get to choose what happens next.

As we create our lives with thoughts, words and actions, we only have to train ourselves to expect the very best.

35

THE PENDULUM

Sedona, Arizona, is famous for two things: its many stunning red rock cliffs, and vortexes of electromagnetic currents there that are rumored to have a magical effect, magnifying the power of spiritual activities. I was curious to see this for myself, so I drove out there and camped at a popular free spot located a few miles south of the city, right off the highway.

After a restful morning, I was thinking about how I wanted to go check out the metaphysical shops to look for a new pendulum, a crystal used for divination. But I also wasn't sure if I was up for it, because there was so much traffic in Sedona. When I had driven through it the day before, the roads were jam-packed with tourists, bumper to bumper. Was it worth it? I wasn't sure. I let the dog outside to do her business and as I stood out there in the campground, a bright, dark blue object on a big red boulder caught my eye. I walked over to get a closer look at it and when I bent down to see it, I discovered that I was actually peering at a pendulum! And it wasn't just any pendulum – this was an indigo crystal with a silver frog charm attached to the chain! I couldn't believe it. It seemed as if it had materialized out of thin air just for me. Maybe it had. What were the odds?

Next I drove south to the nearby town of Cottonwood. There I stopped into a store and I happened to spot another RV in the parking lot that was decorated with big, bright green leaves all over it. You could hardly have hung a brighter banner to attract me. "This must be a fellow nomad who loves plants," I thought. "Certainly this is someone I would like to meet!"

When I walked over to look more closely at the botanical designs, I heard a youthful male voice playfully call out, "Well hello, creeper!"

I laughed. The man who hopped out the door looked young, like he might have been in his late twenties. We had the usual nomad small talk: So what year is your vehicle? How do you like it? What are your favorite spots around here? What other towns have you been to that you liked? And in the course of this conversation we walked the short distance to my camper, so I could show him my own sunset-inspired spray paint job.

And then the conversation took a strange turn.

"What do you think about the difference between men and women?" he asked. He said this with a smirk and a baiting tone. It was apropos of nothing.

"I really don't think anything about it," I said, "but I'm sure you have an opinion."

I got a feeling that whatever he was about to say next was going to offend me, and I was right.

"Men are superior to women, and women are evil. You can even get them to admit it," he said.

I wondered what kind of twisted, self-hating ladies he had been talking to, but I didn't ask. His words sounded more than a little crazy, and not worth engaging, so I held my tongue. He seemed emboldened by my silence.

"Women distract men from the spiritual path. Only men are capable of enlightenment. That's why every great spiritual teacher has been a man and never a woman," he went on, puffing out his chest.

I knew it would only be a waste of energy to bother arguing with someone who espoused such absurd beliefs, so I said, "This conversation is over. It's time for you to leave."

He stalked off angrily while muttering something about how he was super turned off that I was embodying "masculine energy" by standing up to him. (Did he think I cared?) As he trudged back to his vehicle I prayed to Heaven to direct this nut to leave the area immediately. He was not good vibes.

A few moments later, he returned to my door to shout that God was on his side, and the proof was that he had just been invited right then, via text, to visit a friend elsewhere in town.

"It's too bad for you," he said. "I would have invited you if you had been in your feminine energy."

"See?" he said. "I've won."

I said nothing.

"Don't you agree I've won? I'm not leaving until you say I've won," he said.

I felt concerned that he might try to assert his dominance physically, and I didn't want to find out what. He was pretty slender in stature and not at all intimidating to me, but a lot of people have guns in Arizona and I didn't want to find out if he was one of them. So I chose to de-escalate the situation. I hate to lie, but because it seemed like that would be the only way he would go away, I said, "Yep, God agrees, you won." He couldn't see me rolling my eyes.

It was a relief to hear the sound of his engine revving up when he took off.

There's nothing like a hater to remind you of your purpose.

36

TARA WHITE FEATHER

I thought that I would spend the summer camping near Flagstaff, as so many nomads do, but then the forests caught fire and everyone had to evacuate, so I drove east with a group of people who headed to live in the desert outside of Santa Fe, New Mexico. We got into a routine of gathering together and watching the setting sun each night. It was one of these times when a neighbor said, "Have you all met Tara White Feather? She's camped just over there, and she's really so pleasant."

Intrigued, I immediately went to introduce myself to this woman who had the same name as me, pronounced the same way. She was tickled by the coincidence of it, too. It turned out that we had more than a few things in common, but not our age. She was in her late fifties.

As we got to know each other, I learned that her name was given at birth; she is half Cree and half Cherokee, and also a gifted clairvoyant. She told me she uses her psychic abilities to help track down missing indigenous women that the American government doesn't put its resources into finding. I had never heard about this phenomenon before I met Tara White Feather, but it is a very real and serious crisis. Native American women are murdered and assaulted at ten times the national average for people of other ethnic groups, and the crimes against them are often committed by traveling workers in remote places on or near tribal lands that fall outside police jurisdiction. In 2018, the Seattle based Urban Indian Health Institute reported 5,172 missing Alaska Native and American Indian women and girls, only 116 of whom were registered in the Department of Justice database. Thousands of devastated families plead with the police for help and are ignored. As a result, indigenous women have been regularly targeted by twisted people looking for someone to murder. Tara White Feather is doing the noble work of using her divine gifts to help find them.

Tara had a pop-up tent next to her van, and she liked to sit inside it and treat it like a little outdoor living room. As I joined her one afternoon, glad for the mesh screens shielding us from the buzz of hungry mosquitos, Tara White Feather burned sage and struck a Tibetan singing bowl. Then she started to tell me some of the stories passed down to her from the elders in her culture. First she told me the legend of the dreamcatcher, and then she asked, "Do you know why the eagle is special to the Indians?"

"No, but I'd like to," I said.

"The eagle flies higher than the other birds and can see everything. But what's really special is that he has to go through an initiation when he reaches middle age. Eagles live a long time – seventy or eighty years. Around forty, his beak decays and he has to make a choice: Either he has to destroy it himself and pluck out all his feathers and tear out his talons and wait for everything to grow back new, or he has to starve to death. Can you imagine? They have to make this decision. Some of them decide to die, and some of them do it. If they do it, they come out even more beautiful than before."

Is this magnificent story of the initiation of the eagle really true? I assumed it was until one day a friend I shared it with called my bluff. When I researched it, I read that, according to the Center for Conservation Biology, the oldest wild eagle recorded lived only to age twenty-nine, although that could be a low number due to a lack of data. It's possible that these birds may live much longer. The tale could be true.

But even if it is only a myth, it is still a powerful story. I found a particularly interesting passage about it written by a man named Johnny Mannaz:

"During this initiation into a (possible) second half of life, the Eagle seeks out two things: a remote refuge and the light of the sun. It's while bathing in the glow of solar rays that it performs the painful extraction of the old, dulled, calcified parts of itself. Those sharp talons, that precise predatory beak, those noble feathers were once the very things that defined its glory. From its earliest days they were the very means through which the Eagle secured its livelihood. Now, during the molting phase, they become the very things it's forced to shed. Knowing this, the Eagle gives itself over to the solar light and prepares the way for its own resurrection."

I thought of my own journey to the desert, and the rebirth I had experienced.

37

RAINBOWS, MOTHERFUCKER

If you ask her where she lives, my friend CJ will point to a converted horse trailer that she's decorated with jewel-toned textiles, a papasan chair and a miniature wood stove. That's her home, which she proudly refers to as "The HOE House."

The first time I heard her say that, I thought she was making a statement of sexual empowerment, but no. Actually, "H.O.E. stands for Heaven on Earth," she explained. The innuendo is just a bonus that makes her laugh.

What she really means is that she creates her ideal reality with great intention in that little hut.

If someone around her segues into negativity, she'll cut that right off and say, "Speak to me only of butterflies, unicorns and rainbows, motherfucker!"

CJ says this not out of any lack of compassion or awareness of the suffering of the world, but rather because she is vigilant about what she allows into her consciousness, and she wants it to be filled only with love. She knows that how she directs her awareness exerts a creative force and attracts situations that will resonate with it.

For her, as for me, living nomadically offers the freedom to follow the heart, live simply in the beauty of nature and think outside the dominant paradigm, the matrix, which she calls "the sticks-and-bricks life, man."

In the winter we go to the desert to chase the sun. When it gets too hot in the spring, we go north, to higher elevation and take refuge in the forests.

CJ hitches her horse trailer to her pickup truck to move, and often travels with a band of friends. But it's a loose association; among nomads there's a general understanding that all plans are tentative and that at any time someone might leave and take off on an entirely different adventure. People come and go. Nomads understand this about each other and warmly offer friendship without expectation and part ways without fanfare, secure in the faith that our paths will surely cross again down the road – and if they don't, that's OK, too. We fly free, without attachment.

It's a neat thing to see who ends up in your field. We find ourselves drawn to places on what may seem like a whim, and yet those we find ourselves camped next to frequently turn out to be kindred spirits who turn into great friends. Like attracts like. Makeshift villages spring up and dismantle themselves with the seasons. People help each other, sharing tools and giving freely of their resources and skills. It is not uncommon to see folks gathering together and installing solar panels on a stranger's roof, or fixing someone's plumbing while asking nothing in return. It's a culture of kindness and care that inspires you to leave everyone you meet better than you found them.

Free from the pressures of the dominant paradigm, many nomads dispense with the hegemony of the clock altogether and live each day as if it is the weekend. Plans with days and times are always just suggestions, because the truth is we are going to follow our flow, and we are going to do what feels right in the moment. We go to sleep when it's dark and rise with the sun, letting the weather dictate our choices. On rainy days, we stay under blankets; on hot ones, we wake up early and go for walks before the sun makes it unbearable to be outside. We angle our campers so that they cast shadows on the ground that we can sit inside during the blazing heat. No one has air conditioning. We move when it is too cold, too rainy, or too hot to live comfortably.

Some people have their favorite spots for the summer and the winter to which they go like clockwork at the same time every year. Other people get bored and restless when they revisit the same place twice and choose to travel constantly, heading somewhere new and novel every week or two. Some travel with formal groups they pay to belong to, complete with leaders and itineraries, while others fly solo.

As for my trajectory, I can only offer probabilities. I have come to treasure the freedom and simplicity of this way of life. I really love the Southwest, and I expect I'll be here quite a bit longer. But more important than anything I may think is the reality that the Universe has its own plans for me, and I may not be privy to them. There was a time when that might have felt unmooring to me, but today I embrace it.

I've learned to trust the flow, with all its twists and turns.

APPENDIX

Q & A WITH THE AUTHOR

Are you Native American?

I get this question very, very often, and that is why I am including it here. People often tell me that I look like I am Native American.

Actually, in this particular incarnation, both of my parents descended from Ukrainian and Polish immigrants who came to the United States in the early Twentieth Century. My great-grandparents on both sides belonged to the Ashkenazi Jewish ethnic group, which, like Native American tribes, has genetic markers from East Asia, Europe and Siberia. This likely accounts for perceived similarities in appearance.

It is true that many of my mystical experiences and medicine dreams have contained symbolism that appears to be connected to the Lakota spiritual paradigm, even though I never studied it in this life or had any conscious intention around that. Recently, I discovered that there *is* a deeper reason for this curious pattern, and it's connected to the story I shared in the Moon Tribe chapter.

I thought often of the vision I had of the Sioux warrior-shaman-chief[12] with whom I had shared an interdimensional telepathic link. It seemed so incredible that he was *really* me in a past life. Years went by and I kept thinking of this image, and of his face. Finally I asked a psychic for confirmation. "Yes," the channeler said. "It was

---

[12] A purist might nitpick that technically the term "shaman" is from Siberia. Yes, however at this point it has come to denote a ceremonialist/healer/wise one much more broadly, cross-culturally, and is a synonym for medicine person. That is how I intend it.

you in a past lifetime. You sent your energy forward to continue the mission in this one."

Later that night, after the psychic reading, it occurred to me to ask my Higher Self directly, "What was my name in that lifetime?" As the Sioux have been around for thousands of years, I didn't expect to hear anything familiar. It was just a curiosity. Yet the answer that I received was: "Sitting Bull."

I did not know who Sitting Bull was, but I recognized that name, so I did some research. I found photographs of this Lakota Sioux holy man with the very same, striking face I had seen in my vision. I learned that he died at Standing Rock, and that he was indeed a Sioux warrior, medicine man, and chief. In fact, Sitting Bull was appointed chief and spiritual leader of all the Sioux people, not just his tribe, which was a very rare thing. He was recognized for his wisdom, generosity, strength and courage.

Sitting Bull is known for leading a resistance movement against the United States government when American pioneers began to infringe on Sioux land in pursuit of gold in the Black Hills, in violation of a treaty. He was legendary for his bravery in battle – he was known to casually smoke a tobacco pipe on the front lines as bullets whizzed past him, because he so trusted in his spiritual protection. He knew in his heart that it was divine will for him to prevail, and he did.

Sitting Bull was also a gifted speaker. He said, "Those with healthy feet can feel the heart of Mother Earth," and, "The love of possessions is a disease in them." (By "them" he meant the settlers). He also said, "They claim this mother of ours, the Earth, for their own, and fence their neighbors away; they deface her with their buildings and their refuse."

Reading Sitting Bull's words, I felt like I could have written them. I see echoes in the theme of my first book, *Dandelion Hunter*, which is about how modern life has disrupted our relationship with nature. I wrote, "The dirt on which we walk is made of stars," and "Every wild plant is a link to what once was and to what could be. It's all here, still. We have only to remember."

I am more than just this body. I have had many lifetimes. I have been African, Asian, European, Andean, Native American, and beyond. That is why I like what the herbalist Bernadette Torres says when she is asked about her heritage: "I'm an Earth person." Yes, I'm an Earth person, and a star person, too.

How long did it take you to write this book?

I wrote some chapters immediately after events happened because I knew they were important, for example the ones about my ayahuasca ceremonies and my awakening experiences. In that sense I have been writing this book for ten years. But much of the book was written over a very intensely focused two years.

My process was this: I began by writing a list of all the stories, events and ideas that I knew should be in it. Then I dictated each one in narrative form using a text-to-speech app on my phone. Then I got on a computer and edited that text into chapters. Then I shared the manuscript with friends and asked for feedback on how to improve it, and I took most of what they said and applied it. Then I revised everything for eleven months, working diligently until I felt it was sufficiently polished and I stopped waking up in the morning with the urgent feeling that I needed to change or add something.

What advice do you have for people who would like to live full-time off-the-grid ("boondocking") in nature, like you do, in a van or another form of motorhome?

If you want to know where to go, websites such as FreeCampsites. net, Campendium.com, iOverlander and The Dyrt can help you find places for camping. "Dispersed camping" or "boondocking" is what they call it when you can stay for free on public land. Usually these places are managed by the BLM – Bureau of Land Management – or they are part of the National Forest, in which case they usually have fourteen-day limits. Sometimes there are wilderness areas run by state and local agencies, and they may have different rules, such as requiring permits. In some places, the limits are enforced strictly. In others, not so much. The free spots don't have electricity or toilets or anything, so you have to be self-contained. Also, they tend to have absolutely horrible dirt roads that are rutted out, filled with potholes and daunting to drive on.

Typically, full-time nomads live in one of four types of motorhomes: a trailer hitched to a truck or SUV pulling it, a van, a converted school bus, or an RV like mine. Some people also choose to have just a regular-sized car and set up a big tent wherever they camp, though that is a less popular choice. Every arrangement has pluses and minuses to it. For instance, buses and RVs have major fuel efficiency issues, often getting six to eight miles per gallon. And there's the issue of potentially losing your campspot, your little slice of home, when you go run errands, because your car is your home. But vans can feel too small, and trailers can be unwieldy to tow. Many people begin with one thing and later switch to something else after experiencing it.

People often wonder about bathing as a nomad. You can buy a shower at truck stops or get a pass to a local gym where you're camping. In between showers, you can do a sponge bath with hot water and a little plastic basin, and when that's too much work, you can do a lot with baby wipes. Or, if you have a motorhome, you can use your own shower indoors, and if you don't, you can get an outdoor solar shower. There are a lot of options for maintaining one's hygiene.

When it comes to questions of safety, vibe it out. Intuitively feel into the various spots you're considering camping at and settle where it feels good. If something or someone gives you an unsafe or sketchy feeling, listen to your instincts and go elsewhere. I do like having my dog with me to guard my home, as well. However, generally speaking, I've found that most nomads are generous, friendly and helpful. It is very rare to have an issue.

When planning your destination and routes, don't overthink things. Whatever you plan may or may not actually transpire. Let the flow guide you, and expect good things.

How do nomads make a living?

A majority of the nomads I've met are retired people living on their savings. Many see it as a way to travel and keep expenses relatively low while living close to nature. Some find it is a more affordable lifestyle than renting while collecting disability checks or social security income.

The younger nomads I know typically either work remotely and telecommute to their jobs, or they're creative and self-employed, like I am. For instance, I have met a guy who mines crystals and precious minerals and sells them on the internet; a woman who flips land she buys in remote places for profit; two puppy breeders; people who trade in the stock market online, working from their cell phones in the desert. I have also met nomads who do gig work wherever they go: handy-people, carpenters and mobile mechanics; people who do delivery driving; and people who do work-camping stuff like hosting campgrounds, working with horses on ranches, and seasonal farm work.

Now and then I hear about somebody who has managed to make a living documenting their travels on YouTube and getting a ton of hits and thus ad revenue, but that is very rare. Most nomads I know with YouTube channels make little money from it and are just doing it as a hobby.

Where could a person find hapé (tobacco snuff powder) if they would like to work with it?

Of course it is on the Internet, like everything. You can order it online and find unique blends made by the indigenous Amazonian tribes, or by individuals in various countries who blend their own, via Etsy and other websites. There are a number of different varieties of this medicine, each of which has a proprietary recipe in amounts and ingredients determined by the maker. There are some consistent varieties made by various tribes of the Amazon that have specific effects. There are medicines intended for grounding and clearing the lower chakras, for instance, and others that are designed to help you purge stuck energy or open your heart and expand into more meditative states. The descriptions of each variety you'll find should guide you to the best options for you. Just be sure to vibe it out and choose a seller whom your heart senses is authentic and in their integrity. (By the way: Sometimes, you will see the medicine spelled as *rapé* instead of *hapé*. This is just a different pronunciation.)

If you want to know how to use it, my YouTube channel (YouTube. com/@MagicAndFlow) has videos on how to self-administer hapé.

Alternatively, you could hire a shamanic ceremonialist to administer hapé to you. Often people who serve kambo offer it. If you do, you have the benefit of potentially receiving activations from that individual as well as the potential to relax into the experience in that way that comes from feeling someone else is holding space for you. Sometimes it's easier to let go when it feels like someone is looking out for you and making sure you'll be okay. This can be nice sometimes, especially if you feel intimidated to experience a consciousness-altering substance that's likely to make you purge all by yourself.

This is a medicine definitely worth experiencing.

Be aware however that because it's typically made of tobacco, hapé may be potentially addictive. It is also very strong, and can make you feel depleted. I personally do not use hapé anymore. My guides eventually made it clear to me that it was better for me to ground my body through exercise and other means rather than by relying on tobacco.

What advice do you have for people who want to try kambo?

If you want to know if kambo is right for you, ask the Universe, tune into your intuition, and then look for frog omens. Ask it to lead you to a good practitioner with whom you personally resonate and can trust.

And if you sense that kambo is not for you, remember that it is only one of many effective natural modalities. Plant medicine and Reiki healing, for instance, can do many of the same things more gently.

I do not encourage people to self-treat with kambo unless they are very experienced with it already, having already received treatments from qualified practitioners, and know how they react and what dose they need. First of all there are safety concerns. If you do it alone, you could potentially pass out and hit your head or choke on your vomit, or hurt yourself while dizzy and light-headed during the treatment, for instance if you stood up suddenly to try to walk to the bathroom. You could also feel frightened and overwhelmed and end up having a needlessly traumatic experience. Also, you would be missing out on the power and support you get when doing a ceremony with an initiated, shamanic healer who can amplify your intention and transmit a frequency activation to you that propels you into a higher state of consciousness.

Adverse reactions are very rare, and yet, this medicine is not for everybody. It is contraindicated for pregnancy, bipolar disorder, epilepsy, high blood pressure and heart conditions. There are few deaths attributed to it, that said. The situations I have read about were people who either had a pre-existing heart condition or died from drinking way too much water.

It is important to find a practitioner who is discerning about the source of your medicine. Though rare, I have heard of adulterated kambo sticks for sale. I have also heard rumors of exploitative practices among some people who procure the medicine from indigenous gatherers or overharvest the frogs. It is best to find sources who gather the kambo with care and respect for the frogs and of course, good intentions. Personally, I buy my medicine only from individuals who I know that are gathering it themselves, because I want every bit of the process to have good vibes.

Did you ever find a way to be permanently immune to negative entities?

Yes! Eventually, it occurred to me that I could manifest immunity. In this way, I would be calling upon the limitless genius of the divine to effortlessly download a perfect solution into my consciousness, rather than inefficiently trying to somehow figure it out on my own through trial and error. In a sense, manifesting the solution was like using Cosmic Google. So I wrote, "Thank you, Universe, for making me permanently immune to negative entities," and then I gave thanks that it would happen.

I was then graced with an epiphany that there was a tear in my energy field, a rupture making me susceptible to entities. I hired my intuitive healer friend Christine Myers for a phone session – she was also trained in Reiki by my teacher, Jeanette, and is a very powerful shamanic healer – and I asked her to look for this tear and heal it for me. She said she had no experience repairing torn auric fields before, but I insisted that Spirit would guide her, and she was open to that. And that is exactly what happened. She was given a clear vision of a hole in my energy field at the back of my neck and spine, and she welded it shut using Reiki and rainbow light. After that healing session, I never got a demon infection ever again.

Why do you think financial struggle has been a recurring theme in your story?

Perhaps there's no need for going naked and alone into a jungle somewhere to test ourselves when financial stress is pretty much the modern version of a survival crisis. For most of us, being strapped when we need to buy food and pay bills is plenty sufficient to trigger the very same feelings. Though extremely unpleasant, there is value in going through this kind of acute survival stress in that it gives us a chance to really build our faith and develop our manifesting muscles. As my friend Roger said, "You don't know God is all you need until God is all you have."

I know miracles are real because I survived on them.

One winter when I was camping in the desert, a new friend crossed my path who had very little money but needed a lot of help, and I felt strongly that I was meant to assist her. She was recovering from an abusive relationship and she was quite depressed and lost. I gave her several kambo treatments as well as emotional support and many hours of channeled intuitive guidance. She appreciated it, and I was delighted to see her feeling much better afterwards. But afterwards, I felt depleted, and I couldn't afford to replenish myself with a massage or energy healing or anything else that would have recharged my inner battery. My engine battery also died, as if mirroring my inner state. And I had just thirty-four dollars left in my bank account. I needed propane for heat, and I was out of dog food, too. It felt like a real jam. Being so tired, I knew I could not even do more healing work for someone else if I had had the opportunity to receive income for it.

What could I do? I visualized a big bag of dog food in my closet, a full tank of propane for heat, and a working battery. I humbly prayed for help and then I gave deep thanks with as much faith as I could muster. My prayers were promptly answered the next day through the kindness of a neighbor I barely knew when Colin, an ex-biker with a yellow "Don't Tread On Me" flag waving above his trailer, reached out spontaneously and asked how I was doing. Colin is the sort of person who looks after those around him.

"Well, my battery is dead and I need dog food and propane, but that's OK, I'll get it all when funds come in," I told him. "I just don't know exactly when that will be, which is kind of stressful."

Collin empathized. "I've been there before," he said. And so he offered to buy all of these things for me, saying, "It makes my heart fuzzy to help when I can. I can't help the whole world at once, just one human at a time." And his kindness became my answered prayers, the conduit for my manifestations.

Receiving help is something I once would have felt uncomfortable about or even ashamed to need, but I was glad I could do it with humble gratitude, understanding that it is a blessing to give someone an opportunity to do an act of kindness, too.

Hardships can offer important perspective shifts. For instance, on a different occasion when I was enduring a period of financial scarcity, a big well of frustration rose up inside me about it. I trusted that my written manifestations of prosperity would eventually come to pass, but I was impatient with the ebbing tide and eager for the flow to arrive. I felt upset that it wasn't happening fast enough, and weary of waiting. Then I had a powerful dream in which one of my spirit teachers appeared. He was a long-haired angel dressed in a robe with a golden rope around it. He told me, "You're missing some hawk medicine."

Hawk medicine is about elevating our consciousness to find a higher perspective on a situation. The day after that dream, when I was hiking, I found an actual hawk feather, which was further confirmation. So I said, "OK, spirit teachers, please show me what I am not seeing. Expand my thinking."

The understanding that arose within my awareness subsequently -- an intuitive download, if you will -- was that I needed to recognize that prosperity and money are not synonymous. Even though I had very little money, I was wealthy by other definitions, in the sense that I was surrounded with blessings. For instance, I had a home (my RV), it was running well, and I felt safe. My surroundings were beautiful, the weather was warm and sunny, and I had no rent to worry about. I had plenty of food, I was in good health, I had friendship and meaning and purpose and a great dog. And I was leading a peaceful, gentle existence. I began to see that I was actually very prosperous and I elevated my perspective.

Absent the trappings of materialism, one can learn to measure wealth by degree of inner contentment.

At the same time, I would be remiss not to take responsibility for having also sometimes unnecessarily created my own difficulties through harboring fearful limiting beliefs about what was possible for me. I recall an ayahuasca ceremony in which I asked *Madre*, "If you love me so much, why am I broke?" And She replied by correcting my thinking from reacting to creating so that my words became instead, "Thank you for making me wealthy."

Do you believe that everybody can manifest whatever they want?

On the one hand, prayer, intention, faith and the focused use of consciousness are spiritual technologies that everyone can theoretically access. On the other hand, we each have different levels of capacity at any given time. There are people who are experiencing unimaginable stress and crises that render them incapacitated to do anything but merely survive, people who are mentally impaired, people who are emotionally distraught, people who are simply too stuck in the mainstream consciousness, and people so traumatized that they have lost all hope.

Even those of us who have been very successful at manifesting or who often seem to get our prayers answered can experience times in our lives when we fall asleep and forget our power, or when we are under too much stress to do much beyond cope.

That is why it is so important to use our power to help each other. We have been given these incredible tools so that we can bring wonderful things to all beings, not just ourselves. I believe it essential to practice spiritual activism in that way.

Why is it that some people are better at manifesting than others? And for those who have experienced some success, why is it that we are sometimes good at it, and other times it seems impeded?

I have compiled a non-exhaustive list attempting to answer these questions based on my personal experiences of trial and error. This discussion, "Reflections on Manifesting," is in the chapter that follows this one.

REFLECTIONS ON MANIFESTING

T he following is a list of factors that can help or hinder our attempts to manifest, or pray for, desired outcomes. Some are conscious, and some are unconscious, such as our first topic, divine timing.

DIVINE TIMING

Most of us wish our desires would instantly manifest in our lives, but the Universe often has different plans for us. We may end up waiting weeks, months or even years to see our most longed-for experiences come to pass. Delays can be very frustrating, but it's important to trust the process and respect that there are often higher reasons for the timing of things.

Life on Earth is ultimately meant to be a journey of soul growth and expansion. There are lessons we have to master, and skills that we are meant to attain, that sometimes we have to develop before we get what we desire. For example, we may want to manifest a fulfilling romantic partnership, but the wisdom and benevolence of Spirit may require that we first reach a higher degree of self-love, accomplish certain things in our lives while single, or heal old karmic patterns so that we do not repeat the past. We may also have soul contracts that require us to wrap things up, karmically, with partners from former lifetimes, and these can show up as shorter term relationships that are passionate but lacking in true compatibility.

Other factors that affect the timing of our manifestations are astrological influences, as well as fate. We have some things in our lives that we agreed to before we incarnated, and that we cannot change. Some popular teachers make it sound as if there is unlimited freedom to create anything we want at any time, but for most of us, that's not really true. It's more like we get a lot of wiggle room.

BAGGAGE

Another important consideration is that we attract and manifest things from both our conscious and unconscious energies. If we have unresolved emotional baggage and unhealthy, negative core beliefs about ourselves or life or love or money deep down that we fight against, then we may manifest things that resonate with that until we can clear it. This can look like manifestations that seem partially like what we wanted, and yet also partially resemble and resonate with unfulfilling, difficult, familiar past experiences.

In my experience, a mental analysis of the patterns and beliefs is not sufficient to clear them, because they are generally tethered to the psyche by emotional traumas. The only effective way to fully resolve emotional trauma involves divine intervention in some way, through some kind of spiritual healing. In my journey, the most effective technologies have been shamanic healing, intuitive Reiki energy healing, and kambo medicine.

ENERGY CORDS

Thoughtforms are contagious. People who are stuck in limited, fear-based reality paradigms can bring us down and tether us into their world if we connect with them. This is why it is so important to unplug from the influence of mainstream thinking and be very discerning about consuming media. Even if we don't intentionally buy into negative belief systems, they can start to seem more powerful and more real than the positive ones we are trying to create for ourselves because there is so much collective human consciousness invested in them. (This is one reason why shamans and spiritual gurus have often lived like hermits on the fringes of human society.)

We are impacted by our friends and family, too. Through interacting with others or even just thinking about them, we form energetic cords with them. And, through these cords, other people's views can impact us subconsciously. These views can affect our way of thinking about life as well as our own self-image, even without any overt discussion about it, simply because the energetic blueprints impact us. This is why it is so important to limit contact with people who are negative, unkind, or who see us in disempowering ways that make us feel small. (Fortunately it is possible to sever chords to unhealthy people and influences simply with intention.)

On the other hand, energy cords can also be highly beneficial. When we are connecting with positive, healthy, awakened people (and uplifting media influences), the cords between us can elevate our consciousness and help us access a better reality. This is one reason why working with a spiritual teacher or life coach can be so effective – it exerts an upward tug towards the self we are seeking to create and the paradigms we want to believe in.

For example, I recall a day when I was very anxious about something, and Sparrow looked me right in the eyes and said, "There *are* no problems."

In doing so, she was vibrationally sharing a better reality blueprint with me – one in which there are only processes evolving in perfection, solutions about to be revealed. And by holding firmly that her positive belief system was truth, she gave me the opportunity to resonate with it myself, to choose abundance consciousness, to live in the reality of infinite positivity.

Similarly, there was another time when I was talking with my friend Johnananda about my fear of missing out on precious opportunities and he said, "Would you like to join the Always In the Right Place at the Right Time Club?"

"Yes, definitely!" I said.

"Poof, you're in," he said. "Now you'll always be at the right place at the right time."

Belief makes it real.

ASTRAL GRAVITY

The places where we spend our time come to hold the energies of the thoughts and emotions that have been put there, and these can exert a limiting force on us, holding us in a sense of self and a set of beliefs about how life is for us or what is possible. This phenomenon is called "astral gravity." The lightness we feel when we move to a new home or take a trip to a new place is the feeling of leaving that container. If we are working to use new affirmations and change our beliefs, this type of change can be a great asset.

Moving isn't the only way to do it, however. We can also create this same feeling of a shift in astral gravity, a portal to a new beginning, through decluttering, redecorating, and cleansing the vibrations of your home space with music, smudging (burning sage), and so on.

Similar to astral gravity is the fact that we can psychologically anchor ourselves, subconsciously, by the visual cues in our surroundings. If you live in a motorhome like I do, sometimes positioning your vehicle at a different angle so that your view changes can be enough to create the same effect of a new beginning. It can also be helpful to give oneself a "makeover" so that the person we see in the mirror appears to have changed along with our thoughts and our stories. When we change our visual cues, it feels more convincing when we tell ourselves, "Things are different now. I now live in a better reality with positive beliefs. Look how everything has changed."

ELECTRONICS

Electronic devices such as cell phones, TVs, computers and cars are unnatural and have effects on the functioning of our nervous system that can leave us feeling overwhelmed, scattered, irritable or anxious without realizing it. When we experience those states of being, it can be difficult to feel empowered or connected to our Higher Self and intuitive knowing, and thus to use these tools of creator consciousness.

As the spiritual teacher and author Matt Kahn has said, "An overstimulated nervous system is the source of ego."

We can offset the impact of these devices by making time each day to intentionally discharge and ground the excess electricity out of our bodies by standing barefoot on the Earth. Lying chest-down on the ground is wonderful too, especially on soft grass or beach sand. There is a benefit from any amount of time doing these practices, even just a few minutes, but if you can do it for ten or thirty minutes, or even an hour, then it will be really transformative.

GUILT & SHAME

Many of the kindest people have a hard time feeling deserving of the fulfillment of our desires. This can be for multiple reasons.

Sometimes, people feel guilty about wanting good things for themselves because they have been conditioned through oppressive religions to glorify asceticism and feel that wanting good things is somehow selfish. But this is a misunderstanding. Allowing ourselves to receive is by no means a selfish act. When we are truly happy, that is when we are able to give our best selves to this world, serving from a place of joy and a genuine desire to help others feel as good as we do. We can give so much more from an overflowing cup than a depleted one.

Other times, people have trouble feeling deserving of the good things they desire because they feel guilt and shame deep down. We may have a strong conscience and may struggle with forgiving ourselves for times we fell short of our ideals. Guilt and shame are emotional messengers that alert us when we are being hard on ourselves. In such situations, self-compassion is essential to develop.

All of us, as human beings, have limits in our capacity to show up how we wish we could sometimes. We have hormones and brain chemicals and gut microbiomes that get imbalanced and make us moody and irritable sometimes. Sometimes we don't sleep that well at night and we end up being short tempered the next day and react poorly. We may tend to repeat the unconscious negative patterns passed down to us by our parents, despite our best efforts. It happens to all of us. If we lack the ability to be gracious and forgiving towards ourselves – if we lack self-acceptance, demand perfection, and neglect to allow ourselves the grace of being messy human beings – then deep down we will tend to feel undeserving of good things, and we will block our manifestations or limit how good they can be. Sometimes we don't even realize this is how we feel because it is all subconscious.

Unconditional love is the goal. We can't judge ourselves and love ourselves at the same time.

JUDGMENT

Because of the principle of oneness, we separate ourselves from the frequency of unconditional love whenever we engage in judgment. But we can still use discernment.

Judgment and discernment are different things. To judge is to assign a negative valuation to things, to say, "This is bad." But to discern is to observe the differences between things. We can discern between things. We can observe them, and we can comment on our preferences. For instance, we can say, "The sky is overcast today, and I feel down." And this is very different from saying, "The weather is terrible today."

And we can take this concept to the next level when we choose to see everything through the eyes of unconditional love.

One afternoon during my Wandering phase, I got a divine intuitive download, a message that came through like a commandment. It was very simple. God spoke to me, and He said, "Praise everything." That's the opposite of judgment.

As I heeded those words, I realized that to praise something is to send positive energy at it, and in so doing, we actually raise our own vibration because we are one with all that is. And through praising, we help bring things closer to perfection, to Source, as well, by raising the frequency around them, too.

It is possible to see value in all that is. And when it's difficult to see the value in something, we can ask Spirit to grace us with a perspective shift.

We can bless all that is by seeing things in their highest light, as beauty. And to do so is an act of service.

The Navajo have a saying: "May you walk in beauty." The Navajo Beauty Way Prayer goes:

"With beauty before me, may I walk

With beauty behind me, may I walk

With beauty below me, may I walk

With beauty above me, may I walk

With beauty all around me, may I walk."

NEGATIVITY

Negative energy blocks us from resonating with our most desired reality, which is the happy realm of answered prayers and desires fulfilled.

If we are harboring resentments at others (including politicians), if we are giving ourselves a hard time, if we are complaining, or if we are giving away our power to fear, then we are in negativity. If we are engaging in negativity, then we are not aligning with positive energy in those moments. When we are not aligning with positive energy, we are not connected to our Higher Selves and we are delaying or blocking our manifestations.

This does not mean that it is problematic to feel sad, angry, disappointed, or any of the other myriad of negative emotions that are part of being human, however. If we meet any of these emotions with compassion and gentle acceptance, but without creating or perpetuating negative stories, we can stay in alignment with unconditional love all the while. The same can be said whenever we are able to witness our negative thoughts with detachment, without judgment, and without investing in them.

PRESENCE

Quantum reality operates in the ever-present *now* moment. In this paradigm, which is sometimes called "5D" or "the fifth dimension," there is no future, there is no past, and everything exists simultaneously.

Thus, cultivating presence is essential. If we are mentally in the past or the future, we are not right here, right now. *Now* is our point of alignment with Source. *Now* is the place of power and creation. *Now* is where we need to be in order to use our manifestation magic.

Presence is a practice we can cultivate. One way to stay in the present moment is to do every action as an end in itself, as opposed to just getting things done as a means to an end, in which case the mind wanders. When we are able to bring our full presence to what we are doing in each moment, we are fully here.

Another way is to ground one's awareness in the physical senses. Exercise helps with this, as does engaging in pleasurable activities such as smelling or tasting something delightful. We bring our full presence when we want to experience something through the body. And of course, mindfulness meditation offers very helpful techniques to cultivate groundedness. Some of my favorite free guided meditations for grounding in the present moment are those by Andrea Wachter, Bodhin Philip Woodward and Annemaree Rowley on the Insight Timer app.

WORRY

Our belief that wonderful things are likely to happen is equally as potent in creative power as pessimism that things will only get worse. It is up to us to choose which beliefs we will imbue with truth.

Unfortunately, worrying seems to be a very common human tendency, one that the mind mistakenly thinks might help it prepare for an uncertain future, as if things happen *to* us, rather than as reflections of our consciousness. Worrying is very counterproductive. Worry sends creative energy in a negative direction, towards the opposite of what we desire.

Fortunately, there are remedies for worry. One is to "reverse worry," to counterbalance a negative visualization or fearful thought when it arises simply by doing the opposite, and visualizing a positive outcome, affirming it with gratitude, thereby sending positive energy towards it.

Another remedy is to accept the potential of unpleasant circumstances, and through radically accepting it, release the fear of it. A third tool is to distract oneself and focus mental energy on something else. A fourth approach is to ground oneself fully into the present moment, because worry is typically about the future. A great way to do this is to breathe into the heart and bring your attention and awareness there, as if keeping it company.

Whatever we focus on perpetuates itself. If we focus on problems, we create more problems. If we focus on blessings, we perpetuate blessings. It takes effort to direct the mind away from the natural tendency to focus on perceived problems and interrupt its very unhelpful tendency to worry, but the more we do it, the more naturally it comes. It's like building muscle; resistance training strengthens us.

THE HEART

If we try to manifest things entirely from the mind, without engaging the heart, we won't be very effective at it. The heart is our connection to Source. We take the power of our mental consciousness to the next level when we engage the heart, going beyond mere thought to emotional feeling. As one of my teachers once said to me, "Don't just look at the sunset and say it's beautiful. *Feel* the sunset. *Feel* the beauty of the sunset, with your heart."

It's possible to manifest positive outcomes just by feeling good feelings in the heartspace, without having any thoughts at all. This is a particularly clever way to do things, actually, because it opens us up to divine creativity and removes the limited ideas we have about what might make us feel good.

Once, I tried doing an experiment where I welled up feelings of gratitude and happiness and held them as long as possible in my heart, just to see what would manifest. Later that day someone gave me an entire set of furniture that happened to be exactly to my taste and a perfect fit for the living room of my apartment at the time, which was empty. What might happen to you? What gifts might the Universe give that you didn't even know you wanted? Try this!

MOODS

Our moods emit an energetic frequency that influences what we attract and experience. Positive moods attract positive experiences. Thus, we want to cultivate positive moods whenever possible. In a sense, we can then reverse engineer our desired lives simply by making the present moment feel as good as possible. (That is why good self-care is the foundation of achieving an optimal reality. So much of a good mood is just the result of simple things like getting a good night's sleep, hydrating, and spending some time in the sunshine.)

The tricky thing is that many of us are not actually aware of our day-to-day emotional reality. Author Richard Moss writes in his book *The Mandala of Being* about the importance of examining our "emotional holding environment," which is the feeling-state we are accustomed to existing in as a default setting. This is essentially the habitual emotional range we are used to resonating in, and cumulatively, it becomes how life feels.

Our emotional set point is often determined in childhood, at which point it gets internalized as normal, and then becomes something we continue to create in adulthood unless we recognize it and make an effort to change it and make it align with the way we want our lives to feel. We can raise our emotional set point by practicing excellent self-care, getting enough sleep, listening to uplifting music, eating healthy food, drinking plenty of good water, practicing gratitude, watching funny movies, and generally doing things we enjoy.

Of course, it is not possible to always be in joyful spirits, and when we encounter the inevitable setbacks and low points and stresses of life, we can keep our vibration high by slowing down, accepting what is, and practicing self compassion and self care. In this way we stay in harmony with the flow.

DEPRESSION

Mental health problems are legitimate obstacles. Depression is real. We can't always elevate ourselves out of negative thinking or low moods with sheer willpower because sometimes, the underlying cause is bigger than that and is quite physical. For those of us who suffer from chronic depression, neurochemical imbalances, or burnout due to stressful life circumstances, this is a reality.

It's really hard to manifest things when we feel terrible. In fact, it can be impossible. When we are in such spaces, it is best to focus all attention on self-care and then do whatever we need to do to get better. Fortunately there are many very accessible remedies we can use to raise our spirits naturally. Exercise has been clinically proven to be as effective as pharmaceutical antidepressants at boosting mood and treating depression. The natural herb St. John's Wort has also been shown in some studies to work as effectively as prescription antidepressant drugs at boosting serotonin, with minimal side effects.

Often, our diet may be the root cause of neurochemical imbalance. Common inflammatory foods such as sugar, gluten, dairy, seed oils, and chemical additives can act like neurotoxins and make a dramatic negative difference in one's mental health. Imbalances in the gut microbiome, especially candida yeast overgrowth in the intestines, is a common cause of anxiety and depression as well. When anxiety is an issue, plant medicine can be a great help. Passionflower, kava kava, chamomile and hemp-based CBD oil are my anti-anxiety favorite herbs. Many people find benefit from supplementing with magnesium glycinate, as well.

ADDICTION

We strengthen whichever spiritual entities we feed. We feed them through our choices, words and deeds. The ones we feed through the compulsive use of unhealthy substances and self-destructive behaviors are typically not the ones that put loving thoughts in our minds and serenity in our hearts.

A friend of mine was suffering from severe alcoholism and every night he experienced a major metaphysical warfare between angels and demons. Every night he fought with monsters and struggled not to lose his mind. He felt hopeless, suicidal, and in despair. I told him, "When you stop feeding your demons, there will be no more war." He quit drinking, and now he lives in joy and peace.

Getting caught in addiction creates suffering and separation from love, from the realm of Heaven, and from our highest, most empowered selves. Fortunately, this separation dissolves when we return to making intentional, healthy choices that align us with self-love, kindness, and integrity.

STRIVING

Many of us are overly focused on productivity. Mainstream culture tends to promote this through its adoration of "hard work," achievement, and staying busy. Thus many of us end up living at too fast a pace, working ourselves too hard, rushing around in "go mode," praising ourselves for getting things done and checking off the to-do list, but rarely spending time *just being* and actually enjoying the moment. The problem is, receiving requires stillness. It requires time spent just existing, letting the Universe do its thing.

Doing mode is particularly attractive to the ego; it can give us that intoxicating sense of having control over our lives. As spiritual teacher Colette Baron-Reid has said, ego can stand for "edging God out." Getting caught in doing mode can be extremely destructive for manifesting as well because it can make us overly serious, lowering our mood by burning us out and depleting the inner child. It can also perpetuate the feeling-frequency of pursuing and striving, which is the opposite of contentment. We need to cultivate contentment in order to manifest circumstances that make us feel content.

I have gotten caught in this particular trap countless times, overworking myself and forgetting to prioritize fun. I was not receiving my manifestations, not feeling lighthearted, and just generally feeling glum. Stress piled up. I thought I was doing everything right, running necessary errands, working hard on writing and so on, so why weren't things flowing for me? I didn't know, so I took some hapé, sat on the beach and asked for guidance. What came through was a clairaudient message. I felt it was the council that spoke. They said: "It is more important to enjoy your life than to be productive."

This is true for so many reasons, from mental health to metaphysics. The goal is to balance doing and being, yang and yin. How differently would we spend our time if happiness was the highest priority? How differently would we structure society?

ATTACHMENT

When we want something really intensely and the mind cannot stop thinking about it, we get insistent and obsessed and then we are stuck in a state of attachment. Attachment is a way that the ego tries to feel in control of the outcome of a situation, but it doesn't help things happen faster. Actually it does the opposite, because it blocks the bandwidth for miracles – and it keeps us witnessing and affirming the reality of the unwanted situation in the present moment.

My dog Daisy has taught me a lot about the perils of getting caught in the trap of attachment by running away on several occasions. Usually she is very good about staying right next to me when she is off-leash, and can be trusted to hike with me or even just hang out by herself with the door open when I'm out. But a few times, she saw elk and ran after them. It was such audacity for her to believe that a thirty-pound dog like her would make elk her prey. That dog-brained logic, I do not understand. Maybe this hubris stems from the Napoleonic Chihuahua ancestry within her.

In any case, she did run after them, and she disappeared for hours.

At first I called her and called her, but she didn't come back, and I was very upset about it. All the possible dangers out there, like cars and snakes and scorpions and coyotes, flitted through my mind, and I felt helpless to do anything about it. I was very frustrated and upset.

But then I realized I just had to accept that she was gone at the moment, practice faith that she would come back, and use my magic again. I sent up some prayers for her to be guided home safely. I visualized her coming home, and I gave thanks for it. I blessed the situation with Reiki, too. But as a dog mom, it wasn't easy to fully let go and it was all I could seem to think about and talk about with my friends.

Then I saw a horned toad, and I was thrilled about it, and I excitedly went to show my friends. The distraction was a blessing. Once I finally stopped thinking about my dog being missing, she appeared in front of me, as if materializing out of thin air. Perhaps she did.

RESISTANCE

If we are unable to accept our current circumstances – if we believe things should be different from how they are, or how they were – then we are in a state of resistance to what is. If we are in resistance, then we are not able to resonate in that moment with our desired outcome emotionally and mentally. This creates a blockage.

The key to overcoming resistance is to practice radical acceptance. On days when I had no food and no money for food, I told myself, "This is fine. I am still in the flow of abundance. I am going to fast as a choice, because fasting is good for the body. This is not about scarcity, this is a way of supporting my wellbeing." Then I was able to receive money and usually by the end of those dire days, I had what I needed, including food. Because I wasn't allowing myself to freak out and direct my emotional energy in a negative direction, what I wanted to happen could come to me. I was able to stay in alignment with my power, my Higher Self, and thus create abundance.

On those days when I did allow myself to spiral out in anger and bitterness or fear, I only perpetuated my own suffering and experienced more lack. I learned that I could indeed create an experience of food scarcity if I wanted to, or I could remember my power and choose to see everything as evidence of abundance.

The trick to accepting what seems unacceptable is to remind oneself that there is merit in every experience, and also that they all pass. And then, to go do something interesting and fun that takes your mind off your troubles.

SERVICE

When we give to others generously, sharing our gifts, our caring presence, or our material wealth, we stoke the flow of abundance. What we put out comes back to us. And if we forget to help others and become overly focused on our own issues, we can inadvertently block the flow.

It can be tempting to think, "Once I get what I want, then I will help other people," but it doesn't work like that. We have to give to receive. And there is always something we can give, wherever we are at.

FAITH

Without faith in a benevolent higher power, and without a relationship to one, we will tend to feel overwhelmed and alone and our attempts to manifest things or pray will feel hollow. With faith, however, we will sense intuitively that we are being helped at all times, that there is a loving force that supports us underlying our life experiences, and we will feel that if we ask for resources, clarity, or signs about what to do, we really will receive them.

There was a time when I did struggle to have faith in the existence of a benevolent higher power of some form who loved me and was capable of assisting me. I was raised in the Jewish religion, and I met many people in that community who were atheists because they could not reconcile the concept of a loving, omnipotent God with the reality of the appalling suffering of the Holocaust. Philosophically, this issue is known as the Problem of Evil. It convinces a lot of people that God does not exist, because if God is good and God can do anything, then how could God permit something so horrible as a brutal, violent genocide to happen? This argument convinced me, too, and throughout my teenage years and into my twenties I was very proud of being an atheist. I had not yet had any major mystical experiences that convinced me of the existence of something greater than myself, either, although I was always curious about the supernatural.

I believe the solution to the Problem of Evil comes down to misunderstanding the nature of omnipotence in the human experience as regards the deity called God, also known as The Creator. The Creator has the power to intervene, but has given humanity free will on this planet. This means we are able to do whatever we wish. People can be truly wonderful to one another sometimes, as well as truly horrible, and it's all permitted, even things that are very, very awful.

Why isn't there an ethical limit, some point at which Heaven intercedes? I think we really could make an excellent argument that there ought to be such a line, but as it stands, Heaven intervenes only when we ask it to do so. That's why prayer and manifesting are so important. In a sense, Earth is a democracy and using our spiritual tools amounts to voting for what we want to have happen, metaphysically. We empower the divine to help us through our faith and our own free will.

Of course metaphysical law is a complex and nuanced thing, and this space is not sufficient to fully resolve this issue. Nor can I claim to have a perfect understanding of it. Can anyone?

We are each free to define a concept of divinity, of a benevolent Higher Power, that works for us. If the idea of "God" is problematic for us, as it once was for me, then we can use the term "Creator," or we can think of that Heavenly force taking an entirely different form, such as the more amorphous Source or Universe, or as a feminine Cosmic Mother. "God" depicted as a father figure is only one aspect of a massively complex, ineffable being.

Personally, I resonate with many forms of divinity. Often I like to pray to Kuan Yin, goddess of compassion, another female buddha, envisioning myself placing my concerns in her outstretched hands. Other times I imagine that the Creator has delegated my life to a team of angels and fairies and wise ancestors and spirit teacher guides, some of whom come from the star nations, and I ask this team to help me. I think of them planting blessings and clues for me, and working miracles behind the scenes. I conceive of them as having emerged from the unity of all good intelligent forces in the Universe. I talk to them just as I would talk to a friend. My prayers sound like, "I give you complete permission to help me and guide me. Please work your magic. And thank you so much for all you've already done." I focus on using my free will to invite divine assistance.

BELIEFS & ACTIONS

What we believe is true generally becomes true. Speaking our beliefs amplifies their creative power further. This is why repeating affirmations can be useful. The Universe is always listening.

Consistency is important. If we are saying, "I am wealthy," but then later we are pinching our pennies and complaining about the price of things we wish to buy, then we are also implying "There isn't enough," and actually manifesting in conflicting directions. We need to be congruent, or we will tend to block our manifestations.

We can amplify the power of affirmations further by taking aligned actions.

For instance, on a day when I was down to twenty dollars in the bank and had no work lined up, I repeated, "I am wealthy," over and over, and then I took those twenty dollars and went out to lunch at a restaurant, because that is something I could and would do if I really had plenty of money.

A couple hours later, a former client called who urgently needed some spiritual guidance and life coaching, and was eager to resume our work together. As a result, I had thousands of dollars in my bank account by the end of that day.

The key to making that happen was belief. If I had doubted that it would happen, it would not have.

We create our experiences through our thoughts, words and actions. When we do this intentionally, we step into our power as conscious, awakened beings.

I once asked my spirit teachers, "What is the right use of power?"

And they replied, "Unconditional love, unconditional mercy, and relentless optimism."

Relentless optimism.

What will happen next? It's going to be amazing.

ABOUT THE AUTHOR

Tara Rose has a BA in Philosophy from Rutgers University and MFA in Creative Nonfiction Writing from Goucher College.

She remains a passionate nature lover and presently resides off-the-grid in the beautiful wilderness of the Southwest.

Tara offers unique transformational courses in self-love, soul-purpose alignment, Reiki and spiritual empowerment on her website, www.MagicAndFlow.com

She is on TikTok and Instagram @ReikiMasterTara

ACKNOWLEDGEMENTS

My deep thanks to Daisy, my dearest friend, the dignified chihuahua-pit mix who has kept me company while I wrote this book over the years. Daisy has also shared her beautifully calm, peaceful presence during many kambo ceremonies and Reiki healings, and she does an excellent job of protecting, too.

Daisy is indeed the dog formerly known as Petunia, whom I also wrote about in my first book, *Dandelion Hunter: Foraging the Urban Wilderness*. Petunia was the name she came with when I adopted her. A few years after I changed my name to Tara, she asked me to change her name to Daisy – telepathically – and so I obliged. I was surprised by this intuitive message, so I asked her, aloud, "Do you want to be called Daisy?" and she wagged her tail. So I've called her Daisy ever since, and she seems quite happy about it.

Huge thank you to my dear friend, former mentor and healer, Jeanette Hieter, without whom this book would not exist. Jeanette has been there for me during the most difficult experiences of my life, and her loving encouragement got me through times when I felt like I couldn't make it. Jeanette was also the very first person to whom I read the first draft of this manuscript, and her reflections made this project evolve into a much better book. Visit her website at TheDivinityWithin.com

I also send a very gigantic thank you to Lauren Sallinger, my dear friend from the Goucher College Creative Nonfiction Writing MFA program, a humble Harvard grad and the author of *Outside Eden*, who volunteered to tirelessly read many, many revisions for me and offered immensely valuable insights. I am also grateful for the very helpful feedback of Cathie Bell, Britannia Pousson-Nicastro, and

Kelly McCormick, all of whom read early drafts and contributed in crucial ways to the evolution of this manuscript.

Thank you to my friend Jay Beeson for donating his laptop and Starlink wi-fi to my writing efforts, and for taking the photograph at the end of the Rainbows chapter.

Thank you as well to Mom and Dad, who provided me with a fantastic education in more ways than one. I am grateful for their financial contributions to my vehicle repair efforts and their kind gifts in support of my wellbeing, phone and internet access.

I am of course also immensely grateful to my spirit guides and teachers, and to the Creator for giving me such a fulfilling and blessed dharma this lifetime. May it serve the highest good of all.